My Disability--
God's Ability

Justin—

HAPPY Birthday!

Come & See Church

11

11.13.09

My Disability-- God's Ability

7 Principles of Triumphant Life

YOUNG WOO KANG

ABINGDON PRESS / *Nashville*

MY DISABILITY—GOD'S ABILITY:
7 Principles of Triumphant Life

Copyright © 2004 by Abingdon Press

Young Woo Kang

This book is printed on recycled, acid-free, elemental-chlorine-free paper.

04 05 06 07 08 09–10 9 8 7 6 5 4 3 2 1

MANUFACTURED IN THE UNITED STATES OF AMERICA

Contents

Foreword

This is a most inspiring story, told mainly in the voice of Dr. Kang himself, augmented by the testimonies of his two sons. As one reads of Dr. Kang's early life, one is astonished that he could survive physically and emotionally at all. As a boy he lost his sight due to an accident on the playground. Having already suffered the death of his father after the Korean War, he then saw first his mother and then his older sister die in turn. He tells candidly of his great anger and resentment as a result of these catastrophes, and his bitterness toward a God who would allow him to be so devastated. The drama of his story lies in his coming to terms with such loss and his eventual acceptance of his situation. Through that struggle, he found true faith and fresh courage, one thing him to surmount his disability and loss. Indeed, in and through his pain and anguish, he learned to triumph, identifying with the Apostle Paul who wrote that Christ had told him "my grace is sufficient for you, for my power is made perfect in weakness." Dr. Kang is a contemporary embodiment of this secret power, producing an indomitable will and hope in him, and through him offering inspiration to others. It has enabled him to dare great things—impossible things—without regard for the consequences.

Dr. Kang is a living example of Paul's claim "I can do all things through Christ who strengthens me." And clearly has taken to heart Churchill's famous words "never ever, ever, ever, ever, give up." We can all be grateful that Dr. Kang has found such faith, has lived such faith, and has shared such faith with us in his book.

Dr. James Laney
Former President of Emory University
Former U. S. Ambassador to the Republic of Korea

Part I

Nothing Is Impossible with God

The White House, Washington, D.C.
September 9, 2003

The Honorable Young Woo Kang, Ph.D.
8912 Chestnut Lane
Munster, Indiana 46321

Dear Dr. Kang:

It was a pleasure to meet with you at the White House. Thank you for your book. I am grateful for your kind gesture. I appreciate your hard work and dedication as we continue our work to reduce barriers for people with disabilities so that Americans can benefit from the talents of all citizens.

Best Wishes.
Sincerely,
George W. Bush

Prayer

I asked God for strength that I might achieve,
I was made weak that I might learn humbly to obey.
I asked God for riches that I might be happy,
I was given poverty that I might be wise.
I asked God for health that I might do greater things,
I was given blindness that I might do better things.
I asked God for power that I might get the praise of men,
I was given weakness that I might feel the need of God.
I asked God for all things that I might enjoy life,
I was given life that I might enjoy all things.
I got nothing that I had asked for
But everything that I had hoped for despite my blindness
I am among the most richly blessed men.
— Unknown Confederate Soldier

1.

Over the Top

People say, "You can do anything you want to do if you put your mind to it." "There is no limit to human potential." If you had told me those phrases forty years ago, I would snicker and say you are lying. I might even have laughed at you and yelled out, "You don't know what you are talking about." Then, I was short sighted. Now, forty years later, my life became a living proof of all those old sayings that I once despised.

On May 17th, 2002, President Bush invited selected Asian-American community leaders to the White House to celebrate Asian Heritage Month, including seventeen presidential appointees confirmed by the U.S. Senate. I was one of the seventeen. For the first time in my life, I was standing side by side with the most influential people of our country as a member of the National Council on Disability (NCD), which is the senior executive service level IV (SES) or the assistant secretary level position. I almost shouted out, "I did it! I finally did it!" "My dream came true!" It was beyond my imagination, beyond my wildest dream.

Today, nobody rolls their eyes when an Asian-American government officer of some agency is on television to discuss policies. Appointing a minority to a high government position is no longer a phenomenon. However, only a decade ago, when President, George

H. W. Bush appointed six Asian Americans out of five hundred senior executive positions, it did not just make a sensational news story, it became an astonishing historic moment. For the first time in American history, Asian Americans held top positions in the U. S. government. And in 1990, he extended Asian Heritage Week to a month-long celebration. Two years later on October 23, 1992, he signed the bill 102-453 that made Asian Heritage Month.

President George H. W. Bush was influenced by his special interest in minorities, especially Asians. He was the first ambassador to China. He was also an ambassador to the United Nations. He was a director of Central Intelligence Agency, and later became a vice president. Because of the positions he held, he went to a variety of places, met various people around the world, thus giving him a better and clearer understanding of Asian culture and its excellence.

Bill Clinton's administration continued to empower Asian Americans in the United States. In 1997, Clinton formed the White House Initiative on Asian American and Pacific Islanders on executive order, which was composed of fifteen presidential advisory board members. During his presidency, he appointed eight Asian Americans to senior executive service positions.

Currently, the U. S. government employs more than 4,500,000 people. Among them, 2,500 are presidential appointees; but 500 of 2,500 positions require Senate confirmation and are officially given the title "the honorable" in front of their names. In the Bush administration, there are seventeen senior executive service level Asian American presidential appointees, who were confirmed by the Senate. Two of them hold secretary positions—Chinese American Elaine Chao, the secretary of the Department of Labor and Norman Mineta, secretary of the Department of Transportation. I was standing in the White House with them not only as a Korean American, but also as a member of the National Council on Disability. I was one of the seventeen appointed by the president and confirmed by the Senate. Of course, there was a Korean American assistant secretary before me. During the Clinton administration, Harold Hongju Koh served as assistant secretary of the Human Rights at the Department of the State. But he was a second-generation Korean immigrant who was born and raised here. On the other hand, I am a blind man who came to United States in my late twenties and became a citizen in my forties. Yes, the one who once was labeled as cursed was reborn as a blessed one. It was indeed a miraculous day for me.

While standing in the middle of the White House, surrounded by such great leaders of our country, Norman Vincent Peale's words came to my mind. Peale, who is considered one of the greatest religious leaders of twentieth century once said:

"Nobody would be able to deny the existence of God, if they know about the life of Dr. Young Woo Kang."

My life journey would have been an impossible one if I were alone. I am here because of my God. God showed his grace and power through the weakest, yes, me.

As memorable as that day was for me, it was not my first time to meet President Bush. On February 1, 2001, at the launch of the New Freedom Initiative, I was invited to the White House with my wife. Well, the second time did not lessen my excitement. I can't exactly describe what it is. Maybe it is excitement that one can only experience when meeting the most powerful leader of the world; or, it is pure anticipation that I can do so much more for others with the help of the president.

A year after meeting with President George W. Bush, I received an achievement award from the Asian American Alliance for empowering Asians in America. A ceremony was held and Ed Moi, special assistant to the president and the deputy director of the Office of Presidential Personnel, gave the congratulatory address. He said in his speech:

"After through review of his resume and recommendations by the Personnel Committee, Dr. Kang was selected and brought up to Mr. President. He nominated Dr. Kang to the Senate with enthusiasm."

At the end of the ceremony, as President Bush was leaving, he saw me. He walked up to me and we hugged and shook hands. He was so pleased to see me and greeted "Hi! Doc!"

Last time, when I met President Bush, we just shook our hands. That day, it was a warm embrace. Yes, we become more than mere acquaintances. We became comrades in the crusade of helping every disabled in our country. I finally said to the president: "I am pleased to see you again here and also thank you for appointing me to the National Council on Disability.

More than thirty years ago, my wife and I came to this country to study at the University of Pittsburgh, and eventually I received a

Ph.D. Since then, we added two sons, Paul and Christopher. My weakness became their inspiration. Because of my blindness, Paul decided to become a doctor and Chris was motivated to become a lawyer.

Paul attended Phillips Academy Exeter. He studied biology at Harvard and attended medical school at the Indiana University. He completed a residency at the Duke University Eye Center. In May 2001, he married Amy, who is a gynecologist at Indiana University Hospital. They have a beautiful daughter, Aba.

Christopher went to Phillips Andover. He majored in public policy and economics at the University of Chicago. He founded a student volunteer organization, the University Community Center. He also served as a student liaison to the board of trustees of the University of Chicago. Because of his extraordinary ideas and leadership skill throughout his college years, he received the honor of Tomorrow's Leader Today from university president. Chris studied law at Duke University and passed the Illinois bar, becoming a member of the Illinois Bar Association. He works as a council at the U.S. Senate Judiciary Committee for Illinois senator Dick Durbin and married to his college sweetheart Elizabeth, who graduated from Harvard Law School and works at the prestigious law firm, Steptoe and Johnson in Washington D.C.

I want to write this book to tell the world how faith and vision work together, and how faith and vision change our life. I want to share some wisdom that I learned from my life-long journey. Some years ago, I, a poor blind man, owned nothing. Now, I am a doctor and a distinguished senior government executive. Can you imagine what you can do?

Miracles do happen. Once, I was spat on and kicked out of stores because people thought that it was bad luck to see me in the morning. Now, I am a distinguished member of the community. I am in *Who's Who in America* and *Who's Who in the World*. People told me that I couldn't even work in the factory. Then, my only choice was either becoming a beggar or a masseur. But now, I am a senior government official and advocating for six hundred million people with disabilities and I am a vice chairman on the World Committee on Disability.

I still remember praying for a piece of bread and a warm place to sleep. I did not have the luxury to think about the future. I resented

God for taking away everything I hold dear. Despite my resentment, my anger, God had a great plan for me. And God gave me so much back. God provided for me. God sent me his angels. God gave me my wife to guide me through the roughest time of my life. God gave me two sons who are my pride and joy. God gave me friends to help out whenever I am stuck in the corner and don't know what to do.

The paralytic from the Gospel of Mark had four friends who carried him to Jesus. Just like him, I am blessed with so many friends who helped me along the way. I want to thank my friends and family. I also want to thank my God for picking me to be his instrument.

2.

Regaining Self-respect and Dignity

During my adolescence, I lost everything, my sight, my parents, my sister, and my faith in God. Never having a thing is better than having everything and losing it all at once. You wouldn't know any better. Losing everything that you hold dear, it can hurt you. It can hurt you in a way that you can't even imagine. Yes, it can kill. I did not lose just things, I lost loved ones, self-respect, and self-esteem. I lost myself in misery.

I was born in Seoul near the River Han. I still can picture the beautiful place that I spent my childhood. My father owned boats carrying products to Seoul from all over the places. I used to run around the dock with my brother. All my family members were Christians. My mother was a sweet housewife who taught me the Bible. I was baptized as an infant. My dad was a great benefactor to many pastors of new churches. And he also helped many refugees who ran away from religious oppression of the North Korea. I learned so much and my faith grew stronger from teachings of great pastors who stayed in our house during the war. Around this time, my dad's business suffered. At some point, his body could not han-

17

dle the pressure any longer. My dad passed away in 1957 and we became homeless. It was just the prelude to the worse things yet to come.

One day in 1958, I was playing soccer with my friends. I can't exactly remember how it happened. I was hit by a hard-kicked soccer ball and the ball struck my left eye. I suffered from the pain and dizziness for a few days but they went away after a while. Even after the pain and dizziness subsided, other symptoms and complications started show. My vision became blurred and I started seeing a mixture of small blind spots and bright sparks. I got afraid and started to think that I might become a blind.

My mom and I went from doctor to doctor, from hospital to hospital searching for an answer, searching for a treatment and searching for hope. Finally, I got the answer. I was diagnosed as retinal detachment. The prognosis was poor and the only hope was to wait for the retina to reattach itself. I was in complete bed rest for months. It did not work. I had several surgeries, but all the operations and treatments failed. My retina disintegrated totally. Every failed treatment killed me a little bit at a time. Doctors did everything they could, but nothing worked. Finally they gave up and pronounced that I was permanently blind. They told me that I did not have any hope, and the little vision that I had at that time, would be gone soon. Mentally and emotionally, I was dying. Every dead end, every dying hope was killing me slowly.

After my mom realized her elder son was legally blind and there was no hope, she was heartbroken. The last time I saw her was right after they did surgery on me. She came into the fading light of the hospital room. She doubtlessly was seeking for herself some assurance that her son would see again. She needed me to take my father's place in the family. Instead, I projected my anger and frustration onto her. I did not realize her heart was already filled with heart-stabbing grief. Her heart could not take it any more. She left the hospital in the darkness, in the grief of the same terrible agony that tore me up. I think she was shaken up so badly. She was so fatigued mentally and physically leaving her so vulnerable. She died of a stoke eight hours after she left my hospital room. Probably, her last thought was my blindness. Maybe she saw the blind beggar under the bridge, and thought of my future and me. I don't know how everything happened, I just felt so shamed and guilty. I felt like I killed her. Now, my siblings became orphans.

Wonja, my older sister was seventeen when our mother died. She had to drop out of her high school and take on the responsibility of taking care of her siblings, including a blind brother. She worked as a tailor from 6 a.m. till 10 p.m. She became ill and refused any medical help. She did not have that luxury. She kept on going, working and taking care of us. This world asked her more than what she could possibly give. Finally, she died of exhaustion. Wonja probably thought that dying was better than being alive. Maybe that was why she left us. Within four short years, I lost my father, my eyesight, my mother, my sister, and most of all, my home.

I resented the world. I resented God. I could not understand why God was punishing me. God is the God of love. God is supposed to take care, provide, and protect me. That's what I learned, and that's what I read. Instead, God took everything away from me. My younger brother and baby sister became orphans. It was all because of God. I couldn't even take the responsibility of breadwinner. I felt betrayed. I lost my faith in God. Moreover, I lost the desire to live.

Even with the doctor's diagnosis, I could not accept the fact that I was going to be blind for the rest of my life. I refused to start the rehabilitation process. One thing I know now, I did not know then is that God always surrounded me with great people, and his angels helped me out. A hospital social worker to the National Medical Center in Korea, Sunhee Lee, was one of many angels. She made a special offer to me to attend a school for the blind, but I was not ready to accept anything. Attending school for blind meant I accepted the fact that I am blind. I was not ready. I was trapped in the darkness and I did not know where to go. I lost all hope. I just hit rock bottom. Finally, I had to accept the fact that I was blind. What else is there? I had to accept that my vision would not get any better. I had to start a new life.

I visited the hospital social worker Sunhee Lee again and told her I wanted to start a new life. She happily took me to the Rehabilitation Center for the Blind of Korea and helped me to get basic training for a month. The Rehabilitation Center was a small and a private agency for the blind. It was founded and operated by Dr. Byung Woo Kong, the first Korean ophthalmologist. There, I learned that I could become something other than masseur, for-

19

tuneteller or a beggar. During that month, I learned to use the Hangul typewriter and how to write Braille. After mastering basic rehabilitation skills—like typing and Braille writing—I entered the Seoul National School for the Blind.

Even if the tuition was modest, I was too poor to pay anything. I did not have a penny in my pocket. Miss Lee arranged to pay my entrance fee and the tuition for the first three months to the Seoul School for the Blind. But I had no idea where the subsequent funds would come from thereafter. To make matters worse, Miss Sunhee Lee went to America to study and there was nobody to help me. Meanwhile, I met Miss Soonkwi Kwon, a Girl Scout leader at a Quaker meeting. When she learned about my plight, she raised a fund among members of her troop. The fund barely covered three months of living expenses, and when that fund was exhausted, Miss Kwon paid my tuition for a year out of her own pocket. Unfortunately, due to her financial problem, she could no longer support me. I felt my only source of help had disappeared. I was desperate to finish the school. I wanted to give up and become a masseur, which was a common occupation for the blind in Korea. It seemed to me it was a luxurious activity to keep studying. I couldn't even support myself. How can I support my education? I was just about to quit. But God did not let me give up that easy. God has been working in the mysterious ways to guide me.

I received a surprise letter from Sunhee Lee. She wrote a letter to introduce Mr. and Mrs. Frazier McNeill who were willing to support my education, and said, "I sincerely hope that you will become a role model for handicapped." And within a few months, I received a personal letter from Mr. and Mrs. Frazier McNeill. Mr. McNeill was a pioneer of Goodwill Industries, a social and rehabilitation service agency for disabled, and a dedicated Rotarian. Mrs. McNeill was a junior high school financial manager. The McNeills paid my tuition fees and living expenses for nine years until I graduated from Yonsei University. They became more than my financial sponsors. They became my parents and grandparents for my two sons, Paul and Chris. Till they passed away, they took my sons to CFO (Camp Far Out) camps every summer and did everything a loving grandparent will do. They even left a small share of their estate to my sons. Three years after loosing my mom, I gained more than sponsors, I found new parents, kind loving grandparents for my sons.

Even though my financial burdens were somewhat at ease, my mind was still preoccupied with so many strange feelings. I was already five years behind my sighted peers. They were college students. Now, I was about to start a new life in middle school. I lost all my confidence. I had low self-esteem. This feeling of inferiority was overwhelming me every waking moment of my teenage life. And, furthermore, I could not get away from the feeling that God was punishing me. I thought that God did not cure my eyes because I was not a strong believer. However, even in the midst of this emotional turmoil, I learned that God was working in a mysterious way.

I met Rev. Byungsup Van. He was a counselor at the Korean Christian Broadcasting System, and uplifted my life. He instilled the greatest lesson in me. He said, "suffering always has a purpose, and God eventually makes the purpose clearer through individual's experiences." His words reminded me of the apostle Paul. He asked God three times to heal the thorn in his flesh. God did not heal Paul. Instead, he answered, "My grace is sufficient for you, for my power is made perfect in weakness" (2 Corinthians 12:9b).

As with the apostle Paul, God's truth came to me in a flash of inner vision, and a great burden of guilt was lifted from my soul. After the emotional turmoil faded away, I felt free to dedicate my self to study and to plan my future. I was convinced that God had a plan for my life, I was more determined to work through many obstacles: poverty, inferiority, discrimination toward the disabled, and so forth. I strived to maintain straight A's and devoted the rest of my time to college preparation. Several college students volunteered to help me. At this time, I met my wife Kyoungsook who was active in the Red Cross and other service organizations. She played a pivotal role in helping me enter Yonsei University.

In 1968, I applied for Yonsei University, which was one of the oldest schools in Korea. However, the school authority was not ready to accept me, they did not allow me to take an entrance exam. They rejected my first application based on my blindness. Discrimination against disabled was imbedded within the Korean culture at that time, it was not fathomable for handicapped to study with non-disabled.

I experienced another setback, and I was left with emptiness and hopelessness. All I could do was to pray for a miracle. I had a vague but firm belief that God would guide me through this obstacle again.

Suddenly, I thought of Rev. Kwonsuk Kim who was the general secretary of the Korean National Council of Churches (KNCC). During the Korean War, my parents provided shelter for him. I told him the story of how the university rejected my application. I learned later that he contacted directors at the university and persuaded them to give me a chance to take the exam. I took the entrance exam and passed it with flying colors. Actually, I placed tenth among hundreds of applicants and became the first blind college student. My performance paved the way for other handicapped applicants. I made an almost impossible dream come true, and it was just the beginning of my long, wild journey to success.

Owing to this first success, I was very thankful to God. My faith seemed to be revived, and the sense of inferiority started to fade away. It started to dawn on me that God never planned to punish me but had a great plan for my life all along. Vaguely, I began to understand the reason of going through the "hell" of blindness, poverty and being an orphan. God wanted me to be a great role model and to live for other people who do not believe in God. God wanted to show his might through me.

Entering Yonsei University meant more than regaining my faith and my self-esteem. It meant re-entering the sighted world from the darkness and a great deal of adjustment was required. First, finding lecture rooms was one of the hardest things to do. I was bumping into people or scared people away. A few months later, I made steady friends to guide me to different classrooms throughout my undergraduate life.

Some immediate problems I faced were to find ways to study, to prepare for exams and to take tests. There were no Braille nor talking college textbooks available for the blind. I did not have time to pout and play the blame game. I did not have time to waste. I asked fellow students to volunteer for reading the textbooks. And they started to record textbooks. My house was wide open to my friends. On the one hand, these kinds of activities helped me tremendously, and on the other hand, they helped my friends study for their tests. All my professors had to develop new methods to give me tests. Most of them read me questions, and then either I responded orally or wrote down the answers.

Physically, emotionally and mentally, I encountered numerous unexpected challenges that had to be resolved. Nonetheless, I never gave up but went forward instead. I had to find the true purpose of my life. I wanted to show and witness the world that everything is possible. I worked hard.

I did not simply limit myself to studying and getting good grades. I paid attention to my leadership development. My friends and I established a great book club Yonsei Jayoo Kyoyanghoi, which is still active, to discuss culture and books. I played an important role as a leader. I did not know then but looking back, that club helped me develop leadership ability and helped me gain self-confidence. In 1972, I graduated Yonsei University with the second highest grade point average.

I am truly thankful to those friends, leaders, volunteer readers, professors and the McNeills. Without their sacrifices, I was not able to graduate Yonsei University.

3.

Dreaming of Making a Great Family

On February 26, 1972, we got married. If I choose a word that describes my wife best, I will choose the word "courage." She is loving, caring, patient, devoted, faithful, resourceful, and understanding. But I will still choose the word "courage." She is a woman with courage. She courageously guided me out of the darkness into the light for more than thirty years.

I set a goal to study abroad. My wife introduced me to Mrs. Zarfoss who became a friend when she was in the States before we were married. She was a special assistant to the governor of Pennsylvania. She was interested in me after hearing about me from my wife. And Mrs. Zarfoss introduced me to Mr. Williams T. Powell who was manager of a district office for Pennsylvania's Bureau for the Visually Impaired and also governor-elect of the Rotary District 728 in northwestern Pennsylvania. Mr. Powell helped me to get a Rotary Foundation Ambassadorial Scholarship. In May of the same year, I received official notice of admission from the International Student Office of the University of Pittsburgh and notice of the financial commitment from Rotary International District 728.

I was absolutely ecstatic. I was the first blind Korean student to study abroad. My wild dream was about to come true and it was beyond my imagination. I was so excited. I did not even think about another potential problem that was waiting for me. Of course, I was so naïve. At that time, in Korea, in order to get a student passport, all students had to take a government exam. Again I was told that I could not take the government exam because I was blind. Life has never been easy for me. This time, the obstacle was bigger that I could handle. I had to fight against the government bureaucracy. It was a distressing and exhausting moment, but I was not furious any more. This rejection did not hurt my feelings. Self-pity was not in me. I already knew that God had a plan for me. I knew that God would not let me down. I was convinced that God would not abandon me. I had to find a way to remove this obstacle.

I shared this problem with Dr. U Sang Lee who was working for the American Korean Foundation in Seoul. He was an adjunct professor to Yonsei University where I studied. He knew my academic record very well. He suggested that both Yonsei University and the American Foundation should jointly request the Minister of Education to rescind the regulation. He wrote a letter and got the signatures of the president of American Korean Foundation and the president of Yonsei University. The Minister of Education Kwanshik Min approved the request as soon as U Sang Lee submitted it. I became the first disabled student to be permitted to leave Korea to study abroad. Because of me, the door was wide open to the other disabled people.

In August 1972, we left for America to find the great American dream. It was not easy to settle down in a strange country as a blind person. My wife took care of all the family chores. And also she was pregnant with our first son, Paul. Being a first time mom was hard enough, but she had so many things to do on her plate. She totally sacrificed herself and never complained about her hardship. She always saw the brighter side of the things and found joy in taking care of her family.

The Rotary Foundation scholarship was expired after one year. One of us had to work. Instead of me, my resourceful wife decided to look for a job while I took care of two-year-old son. One of her friends, an eye doctor, helped to get a job as a cleaning lady in a hospital. However, another harsh reality soon settled in. We did not know that students and their spouses were not allowed to work unless they were the U.S. citizens or permanent residents. My wife and I went to the office of Naturalization and Immigration and explained our desperate situation, and begged them to make an exception. But we did not prevail. They understood our situation, but they could not bend the rule. However, God always listened to our prayers and provided us with a better opportunity. Again God worked a mysterious way for us.

Around that time, we met Sandford and Keiwen King-Smith. Keiwen was blind and her husband Sandford was a sighted person. We told them our situation and they immediately helped us. They asked, "If you clean our house and take care of our children, we can provide free room and board for you." We were desperate and it was actually a great deal for us. We accepted their offer without a moment of hesitation.

After moving into their house, we realized that our living situation was much better than we expected. Not only we met our financial needs, but it also was a great opportunity to learn about American culture and family life. The Sandfords graduated from Stanford University and did graduate work at Harvard. The husband was a lawyer, and the wife was a teacher. They were well-educated and intelligent people. They influenced us greatly on how to live in America. In addition, our first son, Paul, became a good friend with their children, Heather and Martin.

After this financial strain had been settled, I could focus on my study again. Within three years and eight months, I became the first blind Korean to earn a Ph.D. During this time, I also earned a master's degree in education and psychology, and I became a certified teacher and rehabilitation counselor. My story touched many people. I became an inspiration and a role model for the blind. Ten years after my Ph.D., another blind man, Jaekyoung Chun, earned his Ph.D. He taught me how to write Braille and how to type at the Rehabilitation Center for the Blind of Korea.

My initial plan was to return to Korea. My dream was to be a professor or faculty member in a university. But no job was open to a blind man. The degrees I earned from the University of Pittsburgh were not enough to change the Korean cultural views on the disabled. I was just an exception and something to talk about. There was a strong prejudice against the handicapped. It was embedded in the Korean culture so deeply that no one was willing or ready to give me a chance to prove myself.

To make the situation worse, my visa and the scholarship expired when I completed my degrees. We had no regular income. And our second son, Chris, was born at this time. That put more financial strain on our family. The hope turned into anger and frustration and I felt betrayed by my country. But soon, I realized that God had another plan. Yes, God closed the door I dreamed about, but God has opened a new door to use me for a bigger plan. God always had a greater plan for me than I can possibly imagine.

On April 3, 1976, I experienced a new perspective on my life I became a changed man. Mrs. Crozer, member of the trustees of the University of Pittsburgh invited my family and me for a graduation party. I met Van Duson who was the vice president of finance at the University of Pittsburgh. Mrs. Crozer invited people who held important positions at the University of Pittsburgh: Dr. Maysoner, dean of the School of Education; Dr. Dorill, director of Asian Studies Program; and more attended party. But I was so depressed to enjoy my own party. I still haven't found a job. I had no idea how to support my family. After the dinner, we gathered together around the living room and talked. Naturally, the conversation turned to my concern for the future. I still remember that, out of my frustration, I blurted out, "If I was born into a great and powerful family with lots of connection, I would have been hired by now. Unfortunately, I am not the member of a powerful family. Well. I don't even have parents." As soon as I finished my last sentence, Van Duson said, "Dr. Kang, you just finished your degree. You have a beautiful wife. You are a great father to Paul who is running around over there. Great members establish great family. Why don't you stop blaming things that you have no control over, and start your own great family. You already have great starting members. You might not know this, but I was the first in our family to go to college. I supported myself through the college and the law school. I got my J.D. from Northwestern and became a professor. Look at me now; I oversee all the financial affairs in our school. You don't have to born into a great family to do great things. A great family is great because of its great members."

His advice changed everything. My face turned red. I was so ashamed. I wanted to dig a hole and crawl down. I never saw Van

Duson after that party. But his advice changed my attitude and stayed with me to this day. I could not sit around and mope any longer. Helen Keller once said, "When one door of happiness closes, another opens; but often we look so long at the closed door that we do not see the one which has been opened for us...."

I had to stop looking at the closed door. With Van Duson and Helen Keller's words in my mind, I decided to find a way to have a better life for my family in the United States. First of all, I had to renew my legal status as soon as possible. With the help of Dr. Maysoner, I was granted a one-semester fellowship from the School of Education and my visa was extended one more year. I took nine credit hours to learn more about American education, culture and philosophy, history of American higher education, religious foundation in education, and democracy and education. This experience broadened my view and expertise on education and society. And this experience also helped me set a new goal.

Taking the subject on history of American higher education, I learned an important technical terminology. The term I learned was "northeastern establishment." The term implied Ivy League schools such as Harvard, Yale and Princeton, and the best college prep schools. All of them are located in northeastern parts of the country. In addition, Washington D.C., the capital; New York, the center of world economy; and Boston and Philadelphia, the origin of American education and culture, are located in the northeastern parts of the country.

I also learned about the oldest prep school, Philips Academy. I was intrigued by the history of the school and the philosophy behind it. Samuel Phillips founded Andover, and later his nephew, John Phillips founded competing school Exeter. The two schools compete and cooperate under the same philosophy.

The school motto of the Phillips Academy is "Not for Self." It was a shocking concept. It was like someone just found the light switch inside of my head. I always thought that I was getting education for my success and myself. The founders of Philips Academy said, "Education is not just for us, but for community, country and the world. We are getting an education to show the glory of God through us."

It contradicted what I had been thinking throughout my life. I always thought education was for my advancement. I studied hard to become a professor. Everything was all about me, never about serving others. For the first time in my life, I began to see the true purpose of education. It was not for myself, but for others. If God did not close the door to Korea, I would never know the true purpose of education. And I wouldn't be able to serve others. Finally, I realized the purpose of my life. God gave me this precious opportunity to serve others, including the disabled. It was my turn to return the favor. God wanted me to serve others and show the glory of God through me.

It took me eight months to find a job after receiving Ph.D. I spent the first four months on taking classes in order to maintain a legal status and last four months on looking for a job. Actually, I got several job offers but I could not get those jobs because I was not a permanent resident. It was more frustrating. The eight months that I spent looking for a job felt like an eternity. But that eight months were not a total waste of time. I got important things out of it. I found the vision for next ten, twenty, thirty years. I also learned to see the bright side, even in my darkest moments. But most of all, I realized my wife's unconditional love and sacrifices for the family and me. My angel Kyungsook never blamed me for anything. I could not make ends meet. We did not have anything. She had to walk miles to get groceries because we did not have a car. She used to cut her own hair because we could not afford a decent haircut. I knew it was especially hard for her. She never had to suffer this kind of poverty before she met me. But she never resented the given situation, but rather encouraged me to do my best. She always said, "certainly, God has a plan for us and will guide us. I believe in him." I could get through the eight months of uncertainty because I had her by my side.

An American friend, Richard Fox, suggested Kyougsook to open a store to support our family until I could find a job. He bought a small building that has three apartments and a small grocery store in our names. They told us we could repay them whenever we are able to. They gave us the store without any legal recourse. If we were not able to pay them back, they had no signed documents, no legal trail that would force us to do so. The risk that they took was a material measure of their friendship.

On December 1, 1976, we moved into one of the three apartments and began preparations to go into the grocery business. Most foreign students have at least a secondhand automobile when they study in the States, but we had never been able to afford a car. Kyoungsook would need one to be a grocery proprietor, so we purchased a 6-year-old Plymouth Reliant. Paul, three-and-half, was excited at the prospect of helping his mom sell groceries. I could not see the scenes but picture one of happy moments. I also remember that this warmed my heart a lot.

One week after moving to the apartment, I received a phone call from the city school of Gary, Indiana, for a job interview. Fortunately, the interview went well, and I was offered a contract to start work on Jan. 3, the same day my wife was supposed to open the store. I guess God had a better plan for us.

We moved to Munster, Indiana, on Jan. 2, 1977 and it was snowing. We decided to drive to Indiana. My wife had never driven on a highway before, but she had to drive 450 miles in a snowstorm. We did not have any other choice. So we prayed fervently to God and started out for an unknown world. Paul sat in front with his mom and I sat in the back holding Chris. Luckily, there were not many cars on the highway because the weather was so bad and it was in the New Year holiday time. My wife gained confidence with each mile and it took us twelve hours to get to Indiana from Pittsburgh. Her courage and God's protection made us to arrive safely at Gary. I started to work for the State of Indiana as a special education supervisor and I was able to support my family for the first time.

We moved to Indiana when Paul was three years old and Chris was six months old. Even though they were born in Pittsburgh, Indiana became their home state. I started to work for the State of Indiana from 1977, and later, I taught at Northeastern Illinois University for more than a quarter century. The Indiana State government sponsored my family and me to get permanent residency. This also enabled my wife to work legally as a special education teacher. We both worked hard and saved what we had for our goal and dream. Our hard work started to pay off and we were able to buy a small cozy house. In that small house, through God's help, our family surely achieved great things.

God even provided me with an opportunity to do something for the disabled people in Korea. I was invited to teach in Taegu University in Korea. It is a world-class university, especially in the field of special education, rehabilitation, and social welfares for the

31

disabled. Since then, I worked as the dean of the international affairs until 1992. I made a unique contribution to my homeland Korea through Taegu University.

Twelve years later, in that small house in Munster, Indiana, we opened Paul's letter of acceptance from Phillips Exeter Academy. Paul transferred to Exeter after his sophomore year at Munster High School and completed his junior and senior years there. A year later, we opened another congratulatory letter for Chris. He got admission from Phillips Academy Andover, too. It was the moment that one of my dreams came true. The dream that I had in my darkest moments became a reality. That little house holds so many great memories, but opening those two letters from Phillips Academy was one of the best ones.

4.

Not for Self

When my wife and I decided to go steady, I gave my wife a new name "Suk Eun Ok," which signifies our vision in the future. Each letter represents ten years of our life together. In Korean, "Suk" means stone. In other words, the Suk period was "stone age." It represented the harsh and rough time we had to live through. From 1962 to 1972 we had to jump over many hurdles together—discrimination, poverty, rejections and so forth. I had to fight for everything, every step of the way. "Eun" means silver. The next period of ten years was the Eun period. Silver has a smooth shine to it. To compare with gold and other priceless stones, it may be nothing, but it has its own quality and value. The silver period of our lives was just like the silver. During this silver period, I earned my Ph.D. My wife finished her master's degree in education. We were blessed with two bright-minded sons. Also, I finally got the chance to teach in Korea. To some, being educated, getting a job, starting a family, and buying a house are just ordinary activities. But it was a great deal for my wife and me. After struggling through the "stone" period, every accomplishment was a God's blessing.

The year 1982 was the beginning of the "Ok" period. "Ok" means jade. Koreans love jade because it represents luck, comfort, and prosperity. After journeying together for twenty years, I thought it would be a perfect time to serve others. On the first day of 1982, I myself was immersed in trying to figure out how to spend next ten years of our lives together. In the midst of it, I remembered the lesson I learned a long time ago in Pittsburgh. "Not for self." "Give and it will be given to you" (Luke 6:38a). And "So whether you eat or drink or whatever you do, do everything for the glory of God" (1 Corinthians 10:31). In other words, it is our responsibility to give back. It is the best way to show God's glory. Samuel and John Phillips's philosophy on education is similar to mine. The only distinct difference is that theirs is derived from the Bible, but mine is from my personal experiences.

On January 1st, 1982, I decided to live for others and to give back what I had received. I decided to join the Rotary Club of Munster, Indiana, to serve others. The reason I joined the Rotary Club was that they helped me when I was in dire need. Their financial support opened a new chapter of my life in this country.

To encourage and to give hope to others, I decided to share my past life story. The first project was to write my biography *A Light in My Heart*. The book has been translated into six different languages and distributed worldwide, and also a talking book edition was published through a channel of U. S. Library of Congress. *A Light in My Heart* was adapted into a Korean MBC (Moonhwa Broadcasting Company) television movie and a screen movie. In the epilogues of these movies, President Bush cited me as "an example to encourage and give hope to people with disabilities around the world."

An article of my book review was published in the *Rotarian*, an official magazine of the Rotary International. After my book was introduced in the *Rotarian* magazine, I received more chances to show people around the world what God did for me. Norman Vincent Peale and Robert Schuler also contacted me. Norman Vincent Peale decided to publish an article about my life in his magazine *The Guide Post*, which is published in twenty-two different languages and distributed worldwide. Robert Schuler invited me to his church, the Crystal Cathedral, as a guest speaker for the worship service of "Hour of Power" It was broadcasted worldwide and reached a billion viewers. In addition, United Methodist churches and Baptist churches chose my book in their recommended reading list for their spiritual enhancement.

The Rotary International also used me as a tool to promote its scholarship program. They believe the scholarship program is the best investment for the future, and I am a living witness of its success.

In 1992, the Rotary International celebrated its seventy-fifth anniversary of the Foundation. The world headquarters selected 75 people who have provided extraordinary services to others around the world. Among 1.2 million Rotarians worldwide, I was chosen as one of those 75 service candles recipients. Being one of the 75 "service candles" was a great honor, but surprisingly enough, I was one of five representatives to speak in the eighty-third Rotary International Convention, which took place in Orlando, Florida. I could not even dream of that kind of moment. But it was not a dream; it was real. After delivering a speech at "People for Making the World a Better Place," I received a standing ovation from thirty thousand Rotarians and the guests from 158 nations.

Comparing with what I had received, I gave back so little. I just shared my knowledge and experiences. All I gave to others was a little bit of my time and possessions. Despite my little contribution, God blessed me more with love and with respect from people around the world. Yes, if you give in God's name, God will bless you more than you deserve.

I was also honored by my alma mater, Yonsei University, with an honorary degree of doctor of literature in recognition of my distinguished contribution to the education and public service for disabled individuals I never dreamed of receiving such honor. I just gave back what I have received. But God blesses me more anyway.

Yonsei University

In recognition of his distinguished contribution to the Education and Public Service for Disabled Individuals hereby confers upon Young Woo Kang the honorary degree and he is entitled to all the honors, rights, and privileges appertaining to that degree.

Given at Seoul, Korea
The Twenty-ninth Day of August In the Year of Our Lord
Two Thousand Three.

In witness whereof the seal of the University
and the signatures of the President
and the Dean of the Graduate
School are hereunto affixed.

WooSik Kim, Ph.D., President
SooIl Kim, Ph.D., Dean of the Graduate School

5.

My Special Friend: President George H. W. Bush, 41st President

In September 1990, my youngest son, Chris, entered Philips Academy. When he had to make a choice between Andover and Exeter, my wife and I wanted him to go to Exeter. The reason was our oldest son, Paul, was doing well there already. We thought that we would sleep better at night if we knew his older brother looking after him and helping him out. But Chris thought otherwise. He did not want to walk in the shadow of his brother. He wanted to be on his own, make his own mistakes, and most important, make his own legacy. He emphasized the fact that if he went to Andover instead of Exeter, he would have wider network of contacts. His decision was firm and his reasons were persuasive. We did not have any choice other than let him go to Andover.

September 1990, he left us. We did not worry about him that much. He was a bright, independent, and determined young men. We knew for sure he would do well in school.

A month after Chris left us, Phillips Academy invited parents over for a weekend. For the first time in a long time, all my family was able to get together at the same place. We visited Andover. I had an opportunity to talk with the headmaster, Dr. McNermar, during the reception and I presented my book *A Light in My Heart* to him. He skimmed through the pages and suggested to send a copy to President H. W. Bush. He added, "Mr. President was here to celebrate 200th anniversary of the first President Washington's visit to Andover. President Bush was very proud of signing the bill, 'Americans with Disability Act'. He showed a great interest in the rights of the disabled. And I think he will read it with great interest." It was something of which I'd never thought.

A month after the weekend event, Chris and Paul came home for Thanksgiving. They helped me write a letter to the president, and I included my autobiography, *A Light in My Heart*, with the letter. I did not expect any reply from President Bush.

Another busy month went by and I got a unexpected surprise letter from the president. He said,

"Your story is inspirational to people with or without disabilities around the world."

He signed it with his own hand. I was still holding on to letter like a fool even after my wife finished reading it. What an amazing surprise. Who would expect?

These correspondences were the beginning of my relationship with the Bush family. If Chris decided to go to Exeter, this would never have happen. It was inevitable faith that God planned for me. God was working hard for me, even when I was not aware of it.

A year later, Paul graduated with the highest honor from Exeter and went to Harvard. I sent this great news to the president as a proud father. But sadly, he lost his election in 1992. I didn't hear from him or write to him for next two years.

Meanwhile, I wrote another book with my wife, *Two Candles Shining in the Darkness of the World*. Hakjun Kim, former Korean president's press secretary gave a copy of my book to then President Noh Taewoo. He was inspired by my book and invited me to the Blue House (Korean president's office and residence). It was an opportunity of the lifetime. After the meeting, I received a moral support from President Noh to establish an International Education and Rehabilitation Exchange Foundation. Finally, I had a chance to work with the disabled in Korea. In 1994, the International Education and Rehabilitation Exchange Foundation hosted a conference in Seoul to celebrate the 100th anniversary of starting education for the disabled. In 1884, Rozetta Hall, an American missionary, integrated blind girls into a regular elementary school in Pyongyang, North Korea.

I invited former President Bush to deliver a keynote speech to the conference. He was not able to attend the convention but agreed to videotape his speech for us. Once he appeared in the epilog of the MBC television special drama, "A Light in My Heart," which was based on my autobiography. He cited me as an example to give hope and encouragement to the people with disabilities around the world. In that tape, he said "Dr. Kang is inspirational not only in Korea but also around the world."

That tape was played again on December 3, 1995, at the United Nations International Day for People with Disabilities. His speech touched many leaders worldwide, including then the general secretary of the United Nations Boutros Boutro-Ghali.

Meeting President Bush was an act of faith. Our relationship played a vital role in my life. His videotaped speech touched so many, it opened the door for me to serve more people.

In 1995, I was appointed to serve on the World Committee on Disability where former President George Bush and the former general secretary of the United Nations Boutros Boutros-Ghali and Javier Perez de Cuellar have been honorary chairmen. In the same year, the U.N. celebrated its 50th anniversary. It was possible because of my relationship with President George H. W. Bush. It would not have been possible if he did not open the doors for me. In the same year, the World Committee on Disability and the Franklin Eleanor Roosevelt Institute jointly established the Roosevelt International Disability Award. The award is annually presented to the head of the state whose nation has made noteworthy progress based on the U.N. World Program of Action Concerning the Disabled. For the past seven years, seven heads of states have accepted the award on behalf of their nations. These include South Korea, Canada, Ireland, Hungry, Thailand, Ecuador, and Italy.

One year after being a member of the World Committee on Disability, Dick Thornburgh, former governor of Pennsylvania and the former attorney general, recommended me to be a vice chairman along with himself. Governor Thornburgh was former President Bush's U.S. attorney general and was instrumental in passing the Americans with Disability Act. In my life, meeting these two American leaders has been an act of God. Without them, my unique inspirational and creative leadership would have never been recognized.

One day, I asked former President Bush what makes my story so special. He replied, "Noble human values that transcend culture and language are included in your life story." I asked him again, "What is that special value? He said, "They are faith, compassion, self determination, and persistence."

As I get to know him more, I get to respect and admire him more. It is an honor to have a friendship with a former president. But it is more of blessing than an honor to have a friend with such integrity.

6.

The Honorable
Dr. Young Woo Kang

In 1994, President H. W. Bush delivered a videotaped keynote speech to the 100th anniversary of Rehabilitation and Education of Disabled People in Korea. I was looking for a way to thank him for the speech he delivered, his press secretary told me that a donation to the George Bush Presidential Library Foundation would be a great idea. I sent three checks of small amounts, along with thank you letters. One was to the Bush Library. The other two were to his two sons, George W. and John who were gubernatorial candidates for Texas and Florida. Since then I have been corresponding with all three of them.

Later that year, George W. Bush won the election and become the governor of Texas. But, sadly his younger brother John Ellis Bush (JEB) lost his election. After the election, both Bush brothers sent thank you notes to their supporters. JEB sent me a personally hand-written letter with a picture of his family. I felt closer to him. We have been writing back and forth since then.

After reading JEB's book *Profiles in Character*, I realized that we had so many things in common. We had similar view on politics. I loved the fact that he made his son, who graduated from a prestigious university, teach inner-city kids in Miami. I don't know if I could have done the same. I am not even sure I would have been able to dedicate my own life to teach kids in such conditions. He really is the person who lives by his beliefs and words. I respect him for his dedication and conviction to what he believes.

Another four years passed and the Bush brothers won their 1998 elections, JEB for Florida and George W. for Texas. Both of them invited me to their inaugurations. I couldn't attend both ceremonies. I chose to go to Texas. It seemed to me I already knew a lot about JEB's beliefs, values, and philosophies through his book and letters. But, I had no clue about his brother George. I was curious to know about his personal beliefs and values. I wanted to find out what he is like in person. On the top of that, he was already a potential Republican presidential candidate.

The inauguration ceremony of Governor George W. Bush began with a rabbi's prayer. During the ceremony, an orchestra played Protestant hymns in perfect harmony. It was ended with the blessing from the archbishop of Huston Catholic Church. It was more like a religious affair than a political one. Especially, then Governor Bush's inauguration speech was almost like listening to a sermon from the most inspiring pastor.

"We are made in God's image. So in God's eyes everybody is equal with dignity. Our administration is committed to achieve equality and dignity for everybody. Government cannot solve all the problems. Economic growth cannot solve all the problems either. But as an army of compassion, together we can do. We can solve many social problems by loving one another and by being loved. So compassion and inclusion will be my administration's important values." His speech was more than a fresh reminder of what I already knew. I was in shock. I realized that how wrong of me to assume that people with evangelical faith are only interested in salvation of themselves. From that day forward, I followed George Bush's movements more attentively.

I also supported the George W. Bush's presidential candidacy. I advised him on issues that affect disabled people in the United States. Of course, my personal tie to the Bush family and his Christian values played a major role, but his personality influenced me more. Bush has a very warm personality. I thought his father was friendly and down-to-earth person, but now I know that George W. Bush has more caring personality than his father. He is a real genuine person. That was why I decided to support him. We have similar values and views. But most important, I fell in love with his genuine kindness.

One day, my family debated on various political issues. My wife, Paul and I supported Bush, and my youngest son Chris supported Gore. I was amazed at what independent thinkers my two sons were. Bush graduated from Phillips Andover and Yale University. Gore is a Harvard alumnus and he also lived in the Dunster (name of a dormitory) just as Paul did. Also Gore's daughter, Karenna, was Paul's classmate. If they vote only according to their close connection to each candidate, Paul should support Gore and Chris should vote for Bush. But their decisions were totally opposite. I was proud of my sons who are supporting candidates based on what they believe in, not based on their connections. In truth, even though I respected the Chris' political views, it took me awhile to accept it. I could not just give up without a fair fight. I reasoned with him. I tried to persuade him to be a Bush supporter. If he supports Bush, he may hold important positions in the future since the director of the White House Personnel Department, Clay Johnson, is one of Andover alumni.

One day, I attempted to change Chris' political view through his brother Paul. Quoting a Winston Churchill's famous phrase, I started a conversation casually. "If you are not liberal in your '20s, you don't have a heart, but if you are not conservative in your '40s, you don't have a mind." I told him, "When I was your age, I was liberal just like you. But as I grew older, I became a conservative person. Chris, soon you will become one of us, like me and Paul."

Of course, my son Chris was too smart to just sit around and get ambushed. Chris made the first move. Paul did not even have a chance to open his mouth. Chris said, "How come Paul is so conservative? He is still in his '20s. What happen to his heart?" Of course, Paul came back with a clever reply, "I am mature enough to be in my 40s." Needless to say, we failed to persuade him again.

I am a very persistent person. I could not give up until I tried every possible means. This time, I asked my daughter-in–law, Liz, to help me out. She is an easy person to talk about anything and everything. I misunderstood her polite agreeableness as a sign that she was supporting me. I asked if she could change her husband's mind. But without a moment of hesitation she said, "I promised to work on

Chris' campaign, even before we were married. Sorry, dad." I gave up on Chris and learn to accept his political view.

God always has his own plan. Chris and I think differently. But our differences work for good. Chris' own decision to go to Andover opened an opportunity to share a beautiful friendship with the Bush family. If he did not have faith in himself and what he believed in, I would not have had a chance to do what I am doing right now. Just like Chris' solid connection to many Republican leaders helped me out along the way, my connections to the Democratic Party leaders are great advantage for Chris' career now.

On December 2000, Paul could not come home to celebrate Christmas due to his work. But Chris came home. I received three Christmas cards from the Bush family, one from President Bush and two from George W. and John. While Chris was reading those cards, I said jokingly, "Wouldn't it be great if I can work for President Bush as an advisor for the National Council on Disability (NCD)?"

NCD is an independent federal agency working directly with the president and the Congress regarding issues affecting 54 million Americans with disabilities. Its overall purpose is to promote policies, programs, practices, and procedures that guarantee equal opportunities for all individuals with disabilities, regardless of the nature or severity of the disability, and to empower individuals with disabilities to achieve economic self sufficiency, independent living, and inclusion and integration into all aspects of society. The National Council on Disability is composed of fifteen members appointed by the president and confirmed by the Senate.

It started as a joke, but Chris encouraged me. He said, "Why not? With your background and experiences, you are qualified for the job." I was inspired. As soon as we finished reading the Christmas cards, Chris and I sat down and started to write a letter to President George H. W. Bush. I told him that it would be a great honor if I can have a chance to serve my country and the president. I mailed the letter along with my resume. A few days later, I received a response from him. His response was very encouraging. Even though he did not have any influence over the White House personnel, he said he forwarded my letter and resume to the Bush-Cheney transitional team. At that time I had no idea how people get presidential appointments, and I had no idea how to process the application. Later I learned that the appointment process is a long and complicated process.

On January 20th, 2001, I was invited to the inauguration ceremony of President Bush. It was just a few days after getting the letter from his father. I was so excited about having a chance to meet the president and the first lady personally. The inauguration ceremony and the ball was not what I was expected. It was a real grand event. The atmosphere was filled with excitement and happiness. There was a flaw in meeting President Bush. I did not have a chance to meet face to face with the president. I saw him from a distance.

On that day, I had an opportunity to get acquainted with Trent Lott, then, Republican Senate majority leader. He and I became friends. After the ball, I sent him a letter with the picture that we took together. In that letter I asked him the process of becoming a presidential appointee. Later he told me that he forwarded my resume to the White House Personnel Department. He also advised me to follow up on it. Well, I did not see the use of it, at first. I thought one resume was good enough.

I don't know what triggered me to call the White House. Maybe it was my habit of double-checking. I called the Department of the White House Personnel. I wanted to make sure whether they have my resume. I wanted to know how long it takes to process, how long I need to wait, and what do I need to follow up.

After that phone call, I learned that senior executive positions, including secretaries and assistant secretaries have to fill out appropriate forms electronically. I told them the former President Bush and Trent Lott already forwarded my resumes to the White House Personnel Department. My long explanation was useless. There was no exception. I had to fill out the forms electronically, and I had to start the process from the beginning.

The White House Personnel Department consists of various leaders from other departments and they review every candidate vigorously. Once you fill out the application, every prospective applicant has to go through five steps: selection, nomination, clearance, Senate confirmation, and appointment.

The most important requirement in the selection process is the "recommendation." After thorough review of my resume and several recommendations, Clay Johnson, director of the White House Personnel Department, sent me a letter with a few tips for the interview. According to him, personal ability, high ethical integrity, and high professional integrity are three most important qualities the interviewers look for. I prepared myself for an interview with his guidelines.

Three months after receiving the letter from Clay Johnson, I received a phone call from the White House. They asked me to come to Washington, D.C., for an interview. The presidential council members asked me questions on the health care, education, labor, and social securities. The assistant director of White House Personnel Department wrote down all my responses. I also talked about how my relationship with the Bush family inspired me to apply for the position. At the end of long interview, they told me that I would be selected and nominated to the president.

A month later, around September 2001, I received a book *Survivors Guide for Presidential Nominees* from the White House Office of Council along with the forty-pages long forms to fill out for an FBI background check. After reading 174 pages of the survivors guide, I realized that I just passed the second phase of the process, and I still have a long way to go.

The FBI background check was vigorous and toilsome. Not only did they want to know about my past, but they also wanted to know about my health, finances, mental health, tax returns, and so forth. It took them three months to go through everything they needed to check. Most important, the FBI wanted to know where I have been, with whom I met, and what kind of activities I was involved when I went abroad. Finally, on December 12, 2002, my name passed the clearance phase and reached the Senate. For the first time, I was proud to be a model citizen. Yes, I was glad I paid all my taxes on time.

When my name reached the Senate, I had to go through another background check prior to getting an approval from the Senate. Even after filling out the forty-page long security-related information sheets for the FBI, I had to fill out another ten-page long form for the Senate. After that, I had to get approved by the subcommittee and full committee on health, education, labor, and pension, also by the Senate. I waited nine months. According to *The Survivors Guide for Presidential Nominees* the whole process, from nomination to the Senate approval, takes average six months. Maybe it was because I am a naturalized citizen. Maybe it was because I was nominated right after 9/11. For me, anyway, it was worth waiting.

Finally, the Office of Presidential Personnel called and informed me about the final approval, "Now you are Honorable Kang. Your nomination has been confirmed by the Senate. You are now officially appointed. There will be a White House press release regarding your appointment." On July 26, 2002, the day of the 12th anniversary of ADA (Americans with Disability Act), I was confirmed to be a member of the National Council on Disability by the Senate.

Soon after my appointment, the National Council on Disability started to send me a lot of information. The amount of information was overwhelming. I did not have time to think about anything else other than the first meeting that I have to attend in August. As I started to read the thick reports, I was overwhelmed. I did not even realize how ignorant I was regarding certain aspects of my post. I began to study booklets. I did not want to disappoint my friends. I did not want to make the president regret his decision.

On August 2002, I went to the Washington, D.C., to attend my first NCD quarterly meeting. Still, I did not feel like I was thoroughly prepared. I could not let go of those reports even for a second. I kept going over everything in my head. Even on my way to the bathroom, I had to take everything with me. Basically, I felt like I was a little kid getting ready to perform in a school play for the first time. Butterflies were flying all over the place inside of me. I was so preoccupied with that meeting, I totally forgot about the wonderful event that comes after the meeting.

After the meeting, the White House prepared my swearing in ceremony. I was standing in the middle of the room, surrounded by distinguished members of society, now my friends and colleagues. My swearing in ceremony was conducted by chairperson of Equal Employment Opportunity Commission, Cary M. Dominguez. I held up my right hand up and started to recite the oath that I only heard on TVI (Teacher for Visually Impaired) was repeating the same oath that once every president of this country recited for more than one hundred years.

"I, Young Woo Kang, do solemnly swear that I will support and defend the Constitution of the United States against all enemies, foreign and domestics; that I will bare true faith and allegiance to same; that I will take this obligation freely without any mental reservations or purpose of evasion and that I will well and faithfully discharge the duties of the office on which I am about to enter. So help me, God."

Yes, I was very proud. I wanted to shout out in triumph, "I have overcome impossible odds and made a long journey from despair to presidential appointee." For the first time in a long time, I felt proud of myself. After all, I made it, right? A blind man who had nothing, a first-generation immigrant who speaks English with a heavy accent was standing in that room as one of the top leaders who make federal policies that affects millions of people.

In part, I was thankful to my friends and family who supported me through thick and thin. Especially, I felt indescribable gratitude toward my wife. Because, I knew one thing for sure, I knew that without her help and support I wouldn't be able to stand where I was standing. I was grateful to my God. I was thankful and all that when I first received the phone call from the Office of Presidential Personnel. At first, I was grateful to my God for leading me to the NCD. But it was little bit different this time. Maybe I finally could feel the weight of the great journey that I was just about to embark. This time, I was grateful for giving me the ultimate chance to serve disabled people all around this country. Yes, God is using his small and partially broken tool Young Woo to do his great works, again.

George W. Bush, President of the United States

To all who shall see these presents, Greetings;

Know ye, that reposing whereas trust and confidence in the Integrity and ability of Young Woo Kang, of Indiana. I have nominated, and by and with the advice and consents of the Senate, do appoint him as a member of the National Council on Disability for a term expiring September 27, 2006, and do authorize and empower him to execute and fulfill the duties of that Office according to law: and to have and to held the said Office, with all the powers, privileges and emoluments thereunto of right appertaining, unto him the said Young Woo Kang, subject to the conditions prescribed by law.

In testimony whereof, I have caused these letters to be made. Patent and the Seal of the United States to be hereunto affixed.

Done at the City of Washington this Twenty-Ninth Day of July, in the year of our Lord Two Thousand Two.

And of the Independence of the United States of America the two hundred and twenty seventh

By the President

Secretary of State

Part II

Story of Two Sons

7.

A Family of Stars

The healing of the world is in its nameless saints. Each separate star seems nothing. But a myriad of scattered stars breaks up the night and makes it beautiful.   *(Bayard Taylor)*

Introduction

To tell you the truth, I always have been uncomfortable writing stories for my father's books because I'm not sure that I have anything to write that would be worth reading. I mean, what did I have to offer as an 18-year-old high school graduate? Or even as a law school student who had yet to set foot in the real world? But despite years of protest, I nonetheless fulfilled the role of dutiful son and wrote a few pages for my father, swearing each time would be the last.

But, of course, here I am again—even though I'm still not convinced I have all that much to offer at the grand old age of 27. So why write? Because for once, I have control over what will be published. In the past, my father has translated—and (dare I say?) possibly embellished—my stories; since my grasp of Korean isn't all that great, I actually have no idea what's in those translated versions. So

51

this is my grand opportunity to set the record straight. Get ready for Chris Kang: uncensored. (You can tell the difference already—the translated version would have said "Chris Kang, J.D.: uncensored" because my father likes to throw in my law degree every chance he gets.)

Not that "uncensored" will mean anything particularly exciting or revealing—perhaps just some control over the style and structure of my stories. I also thought I would take this opportunity to include some new material, instead of just the English version of stories you have already read or heard. So, without further ado, here are stories that embody the people who have influenced my life the most: my family. Oh, and since I have your attention, I'm also hopping on my soapbox and including a speech I gave to the Korean Youth Center of New York about the future of Korean Americans. (Looks like I may have something to include that's worth reading after all, eh?)

Making Change

I know this will make me sound like a big nerd, but one of my favorite memories of growing up with my father was a game we played called "Making Change." He would ask, "How many ways can you make 87 cents?" And I would run to my room and start scribbling a list:
3 Quarters, 1 Dime, 2 pennies
3 Q, 2 N, 2 P
3 Q, 12 P
2 Q, 3 D, 1 N, 2 pennies
and so on, until I had written down all of the possibilities. I would then run back to my father with the answer and get another amount of money from him to play again.

After a couple days, I got to four or five dollars, and I had learned a few things. First, the purpose of the game was to teach me to approach problems logically. When I started, I would list the possibilities in the order they came to mind. For example, for 30 cents, I would start with 30 pennies, then a quarter and a nickel, then three dimes, and so on. But I would miss something or spend a lot of time going over my list to make sure I had them all. After a few tries, I realized that I had to start by using quarters first, exhaust all of the possibilities, and then move on to using as many dimes as possible, and so on.

This game taught me that there are many ways to approach a situation. If you don't have three dimes, try to scrounge up two dimes and a couple nickels; there's always another way.

Those are the lessons my father intended for me to master, but I learned an even greater one that day. I realized that my father was playing along by keeping his list—no matter how long—in his head, and it is one of my first memories of truly understanding that my father's blindness was not a disability. In retrospect, of course, this game was nothing compared to earning a Ph.D., but I had no idea what it took to get a doctoral degree. What I did know what that my father could keep a list of dozens of possibilities in his mind and recall them just as easily as I could read them from my hastily-written sheets of paper; he clearly didn't need to see to play along.

As I grew older, I learned that not only was my father's blindness not a disability, but through courage, faith, and determination, he had transformed it into an asset. My father has taught me that each of us has limitless potential if only given the opportunity and that each person can open doors for others to enter and thereby change the world.

For as long as I can remember, my father has said to my brother and me, "I am a blind immigrant in a new country. As second-generation Korean Americans, you must do more than me." And so, I have dedicated my life to reaching that standard—to making change and to having as great an impact on the world as my father. My hope is to provide the opportunity for as many people as possible to explore their potential and to reach their dreams. But sometimes, I just wish my father would stop raising that bar; it's going to be hard enough to be a presidential appointee—who knows what I will have to top next.

The Heart of Our Family

I had one of my first organized volunteer experiences in high school, when I helped my mother teach in a summer school for visually impaired students in Gary, Indiana. As I worked with these students and taught them how to use special computer programs, I fell in love with volunteerism. But it was not only the joy of seeing that spark in the students' faces as they learned something new. For the first time, I saw the passion my mother has for helping others—not to mention how good she is at it—and I wanted to share that feeling.

My mother has been just as tireless an advocate for people with disabilities as my father. In 2004, she will retire after teaching visually impaired students for almost twenty-eight years. Her dedication and love of others, while always present, is even clearer in the classroom, as she provides her students with mobility skills and a sense of freedom. Since that summer, I have tried to emulate her and to take the initiative to help others in need.

Take college, for example. The University of Chicago is uniquely situated as a center of wealth in the midst of poverty in Chicago's South Side. I wanted to better integrate the university and its surrounding neighborhoods into one larger community, so I worked with others to create service opportunities, such as a reading program for preschool children. I also was active in the university community and served in student government for two years. I helped create a yearbook, improved campus safety, and raised money for local charities.

Although my grades admittedly suffered from all the time I devoted to these activities, my mother was always supportive. She had taught me that I have the power to improve the lives of those around me and that I should take advantage of every opportunity I have to use that power. After all, when she was a student, she took the chance to help a young blind man, and things have turned out pretty well for them.

I like to think that while my father is the head of our family, my mother has always been there as our heart, and I hope to follow in her love, compassion, and dedication.

Warning: Do Not Try This at Home

As I lay on the ground, gasping for air, I could hear my brother calling out to me, "Chris! You didn't roll! You have to roll, man!"

I was about ten years old, and I had just had the wind knocked out of me, because apparently I did not roll—after I jumped off the roof of our garage.

Now, jumping off that roof is not quite as crazy as it sounds (although I still wouldn't recommend it to anyone). It's not as if I was pretending to be Superman and thought I could fly. Oh no. I was pretending to be MacGyver, the everyman's hero who relied on science and a pocketknife as his weapon. Paul thought he would use MacGyver to teach me a little physics and the fact that if you rolled as you hit the ground, the force of your impact would be dispersed, and you wouldn't get hurt. Since I was pretty sure that even MacGyver made up some things for television (how many different uses can there really be for a stick of gum?), my brother decided to demonstrate first. He jumped off the roof, rolled as he hit the ground, and popped right up. See? Nothing to it.

I, on the other hand, was so scared of the ground as I hurled toward it, that I forgot to roll. Luckily, the roof wasn't very high, and I only had the wind knocked out of me. But I did learn a few important things that day. One, my brother was crazy, and I shouldn't try to do everything he did. (I didn't fully grasp this lesson until a few years later, when I cut my chin open trying to do an "easy" skateboard trick he taught me.) Two, my brother was crazy, and I loved and admired that about him.

Give or take a few bumps and bruises, my brother has always been the ultimate role model. As long as he understands the theory behind something, he has never been afraid to try it. Like jumping off the roof. Or pole-vaulting. Or parasailing. What's more, Paul is able to put in the time and effort to master whatever he tries. From art and music to sports and medicine, he has done it and done it well.

I, on the other hand, have always been the risk-averse one—more content to sit in bed with a good book than oh, say, jump off the roof of the garage. Among the many lessons I have learned from my brother is the adage: "Nothing ventured, nothing gained." He has taught me not only to take the leap into something new, but also to make sure I try my hardest once I do.

Today is a special day for Paul and the rest of our family—it's December 30, 2003, and a few hours ago, I become an uncle. I know Paul is going to be a great father who will pass on these lessons and more to his children. I just hope they talk to their Uncle Chris before trying any ideas they get from MacGyver reruns.

Following God's Plan

If you have ever read my father's books or heard him speak, you probably know about my sixth-grade autobiography. It took an entire semester to write, and while the early years were nonfiction, it also had chapters on high school, college, and beyond. Of course, many of my fictional predictions did not come true. For example, my brother did not catch a game-winning touchdown for the Princeton Tigers, and I did not move to Pittsburgh to practice law. But one thing was surprisingly close. In my autobiography, I married my college girlfriend on my birthday: June 15, 2001; in reality, I married my college girlfriend on my birthday—except it was June 15, 2002.

To be perfectly honest, though, it's a bit of a stretch to call Elizabeth my college girlfriend. Technically, we did start dating while we were in college. It was Senior Week, the week after finals had ended but before graduation—a week for seniors to celebrate and to spend a few final days with the friends they have made over the past four years. Clearly, it was a time for goodbyes, not hellos. And yet there we were, in the early hours of Friday morning—the day before graduation—taking in a sunrise over Lake Michigan and charting a new course for the rest of our lives.

During Senior Week, Elizabeth and I tried to spend as much time as possible with our friends—including several mutual ones—which meant we bumped into each another a lot more than we had in the past. On Thursday night, our group decided that we would finally—after years of failed attempts—watch the sun rise.

As we stretched out on the rocky shore, I moved closer to the water, so I could see how warm it was. A few moments later, Elizabeth walked toward me and struck up a conversation. Four hours later, with the sun high in the sky, we were alone on the shore—still talking away—and I knew she was the woman I was going to marry. I also knew I was a hopeless romantic and that actually marrying her was highly unlikely—after all, I was probably headed to law school in the fall, while she would stay and work in Chicago for at least a year.

Even after an amazing summer packed with two or three dates a week and hours on the phone in between, all logic pointed to ending our relationship when I moved to North Carolina for law school. We had both been in long-distance relationships before and were wary of trying another. But we decided to pray about and to take it one day at a time. And after a four-year long-distance relationship, we got married.

It just goes to show that regardless of logic, if God has a plan for you, you have to go with your heart and follow His plan. Elizabeth has not only helped to deepen my faith, but she also challenges me to be a better person, while at the same time accepting me for who I am and allowing me to be myself. She has been an amazing partner, and I cannot imagine being more blessed.

My Soapbox: Korean Americans for the Next 100 Years (from a speech I gave to the Korean Youth Center of New York on May 17, 2003.)

This year is the centennial of the arrival of Korean immigrants in the United States. Over the past one hundred years, my parents, along with yours, or your grandparents or even yourselves came to this country in search of better lives for themselves and for us.

That is amazing. I cannot even begin to imagine packing my bags and starting over in another country—not even England or Canada. And yet, our families made those sacrifices for us. So as we look back over the past one hundred years, we need to not only celebrate our accomplishments, but also look back at those sacrifices. To show our respect and gratitude in recognition of what it took to be here today, we must commit ourselves to fulfilling the dreams our parents had for us: that we be successful in this society. As we look to the future and the next one hundred years, I strongly believe our path to success must involve public service and political activism.

Our parents have taken a very traditional and straightforward path to success: hard work, determination, and education. And they have passed those virtues on to us—constantly pushing us to work harder and to do better.

While those things are still necessary to succeed, I don't think that's enough for us. It's not all about "Study, study, study." Success is about being a contributing member of this society, and public service, politics, and community are huge components of that. I know that with classes and parental pressure, service sometimes takes a back seat in your hectic schedules. But I would like to encourage you to give it a try. Because when you start giving of yourself, you receive so much back that you'll have a hard time trying to keep service at the bottom of your list.

There are many reasons to get started in public service—some more altruistic than others. Here are just a few of the reasons I've been involved. I'm driven by my Christian faith. In high school, I learned that my name "Christopher" means "Christ bearing," and I have taken that responsibility to heart. As I have embarked on my own personal pursuit of "What would Jesus do?" I've come to believe that Jesus would be volunteering at a soup kitchen or mentoring children.

While in college, I saw firsthand poverty in surrounding neighborhoods, and I thought, "I should do what I can to help these people to at least get the opportunity to succeed."

I have had good role models. For example, one of my first volunteer experiences in high school was helping my mom, as she taught summer school to visually impaired students in Gary, Indiana. And then there are the more selfish reasons to be involved in public service:

It looks good on your college application and your resume.

In high school, there was a cute girl who was working on a community service project and asked me to help out.

All of these reasons played a role in my getting started in public service. But in the end, one thing has kept me going throughout the years so that I have made a career out of it: the almost addictive joy you get from helping others and watching your actions have a positive effect on their lives.

In college, one of my first formal volunteer experiences was with a job-training program for high school graduates from low-income families. One of my jobs was intake. We would administer tests to determine their reading level, and we would determine their skills and interests. It was thrilling to watch these young men and women taking the necessary steps to find good jobs that could pay their bills.

But at the same time, it was heartbreaking. We had to turn away many students because they tested at lower than a sixth grade reading level. Why was that? They had graduated from high school and were trying to do the right thing. They had put in twelve years of school but somehow came out with less than six years of education. Clearly, something was wrong with the system, and I took it upon myself to take action.

I learned that in order to succeed in school, one of the greatest assets—and one I had taken for granted—is having someone read to you when you are young. Those parents who work two or three jobs a day to pay to the bills and to put food on the table don't always have time to read to their children. So a few friends and I started a reading program for preschool children, to work on their reading skills and to show them that reading can be fun.

I also put my experiences to work in the classroom, and I wrote my public policy thesis on Illinois's public schools. I learned that the amount of money spent on each student depended largely on where he or she lived, and that a law that would have reduced this dispar-ity had unfortunately failed. I began to understand the power of gov-ernment and the ability of even one law to make a difference in the lives of thousands of people. So, all of this led me to government and to politics.

Today, I am counsel for Senator Richard Durbin, and one of the most striking things in my job has been noticing how few Asian Americans work in Capitol Hill. A key reason for this is the lack of role models. There just haven't been many Asian Americans who have taken the path of public service and ended up in politics and government.

I understand that especially as Korean Americans, we are con-fronted with the stigma of politics. I remember reading a *New York Times* article about politics in South Korea that said, "For nearly half a century, corruption has been as Korean as kimchi." Here in the United States, the only Korean American representative in Congress served for three terms before pleading guilty to fund-rais-ing violations. So I understand the cultural resistance to politics.

But that is not politics. The late Sen. Paul Wellstone from Minnesota—one of my political heroes and role models—once said, "Politics is not about money and power games. It is about improv-ing people's lives, about making our country better."

Over the past ten years, Korean Americans have learned this truth and are becoming more politically active. I think one of the reasons for this change in attitude is the Los Angeles riots in 1992. For many Korean Americans older than me, these events, known as "Sa-I-Gu" for April 29, were a defining realization that politics are important. That being successful in a small business or in a small community is not sufficient without being part of the broader community and the political process as a whole.

For me, that was not a defining moment. In 1992, I was a high school sophomore, still trying to make sense of my Korean-American identity. In fact, I still am.

But because of the progress Korean Americans have made in becoming more politically active, we will not have another eye-open-ing event such as Sa-I-Gu. However, in the absence of such an event, we, as younger Korean Americans, must use a different way to find our path into politics; I believe that way will be finding our Korean-American identity and realizing its importance.

As someone who grew up in an almost all-white town, I did not have a strong sense of Korean culture and Korean-American identity. I mean, my parents passed on traditions and culture, but I still spent a lot of my youth trying to fit in. To assimilate.

It wasn't until I came to Capitol Hill that my Asian-American identity and the importance of being an Asian American really hit me. Since Asian Americans are underrepresented in staff and in lobbying Congress, we do not have a seat at that table when policies affecting our lives are debated and enacted.

That is what must change. So, what is the take-home message today? Success for Korean Americans in the next one hundred years will revolve around three concepts that we as a community have not given as much consideration to in the past: public service, politics, and community. But I want you to bear in mind that these are very broad concepts.

What is your community? The Korean community? The Korean-American community? Your church? Your school? Flushing? Consider, as you contribute to your community, breaking down the traditional boundaries that separate us. For example, in college, I worked to integrate the university with its surrounding neighborhoods into one larger community. I challenge you to break down barriers and to build coalitions—between Asian Americans, between minorities, between people of different faiths.

I also urge you to consider public service as broadly as possible. My full-time job happens to be in government. But I am constantly reminded how broad public service is when I see my wife, who is a lawyer in a private law firm, volunteer as a mentor once a week. Public service does not have to be a full-time job. But it does have to part of your life. Whatever your occupation—whether it is student, parent, doctor, cashier—you must engage in public service. Society is not a one-way street. In order for Korean Americans to achieve success in today's society, we must be willing to make contributions back to society.

Finally, political activism. My job in the United States Congress doesn't get more politically active. But activism takes many forms. Register to vote. And then actually vote. Read the newspaper and study the issues. Build coalitions to strengthen your voice and to lobby for change. Politics should not be divided by party. Senator Wellstone said, "Politics is not about left, right, or center. It is about speaking to the concerns and circumstances of people's lives." That is truly what politics is about and why we, as Korean Americans must be involved in politics. This diversity in politics will certainly help us in the long run, as we have a voice in government.

But this encouragement is not only based in self-interest. Diversity benefits government as well. We each—personally and collectively—bring different voices and life experiences to politics. And the process benefits from all of these viewpoints being expressed and considered.

I would like to close with something my father often said to me as I grew up. He said, "I am a blind immigrant in a new country. As a second-generation Korean American, you must do better." Although he has set that bar rather high, I am working to achieve that goal, and I urge you to do the same. Through public service, community, and politics, we can fulfill our parents' dreams of being more successful, and more importantly, we will blaze a path for others to follow so that our children, too, can be more successful than us.

Conclusion: A Family of Stars

For all the times I have written stories for these books, I have to admit that I still don't really know what my father is looking for. "Stories about your life," he always says. Well, with only a couple years of real world experience under my belt, those stories aren't likely to be very exciting. Sure, I could throw in some of my accomplishments from college or law school. But, one, I think that would read like a résumé, and, two, I'm sure my father has already tossed enough of those in.

So, I thought I would at least give you a glimpse into the greatest influences in my life and what I have learned from them. In doing so, I hope to illuminate each of these stars so they not only shine brightly on their own, but so that you can see how they have combined to make my life beautiful.

Christopher D. Kang, J.D., Council at US Senate Judiciary Committee for Senator Dick Durbin

My Wonderful Dreams Came True

The healing of the world is in its nameless saints. Each separate star seems nothing. But a myriad of scattered stars breaks up the night and makes it beautiful.
(Bayard Taylor)

Introduction

Growing up with a blind father, I had always felt a desire to help with his condition. I can remember as a young child, praying to God to let my father see. Then in elementary school, I vowed to invent a car that was voice activated so that my father could drive and would be less dependent upon my mother. After wrestling with many different ideas throughout my youth, I settled on becoming an eye doctor; and now that childhood dream has become a reality. After graduating from Phillips Exeter Academy, Harvard University, and Indiana University School of Medicine, I recently finished my residency in ophthalmology at Duke University.

Every journey has its story. As I look back at my life, I wonder how I arrived at this destination. What happened to make this dream come true, and what have I learned along the way? My life is not a story of success that came easy. It is full of both victories and disappointments; much laughter and tears.

However, what I have come to realize is that my success has come from a combination of talent, determination, family support, and good fortune. All four of these elements throughout my life have been crucial toward achieving my dream, and absent one of them, I am convinced the story would have turned out differently. My life is by no means meant to be a prescription for success, it is simply an illustration of what I believe can happen when a person maximizes their abilities, is surrounded by a tremendous support system, and has some good luck. Here is my story.

My parents have always told me that I was a precocious child. They say that I spoke phrases at the age of ten months, and took my first steps at eleven months. Although I don't remember any of these childhood milestones, I do remember my parents always calling me "gifted" and loving to showcase my talents. My dad would have me count to ten in English, Korean, Spanish, and Hebrew. Then he would have me read aloud to guests. He even recorded many of these sessions on audiotape.

My memories of formal education began at James B. Eads elementary school in Munster, Indiana. There I started in first grade and admit that at the time studying was not my main priority. Even though my parents emphasized education, my favorite subjects were gym, music, art, and math. I included math as one of my favorites, because we had timed tests, and I would always race with my friends to finish first, not really caring if my answers were correct. I can only speculate why I did not enjoy the fundamental subjects like reading, spelling, and English. Perhaps I preferred the creative aspects of the fine arts or maybe I was just too distracted with other activities to pay attention in class.

Regardless, report card day was never really a happy time for me. During elementary school, the ritual was the same. The academic grades would always be slightly above average, the behavior grades would be average, and the teacher comments would read, "Paul talks too much. He spends too much time mingling with friends and too little time paying attention in class." Inevitably, my parents would be upset and as an extension I was upset. I would come home and hand over my report card. Then my parents would give me lecture about the importance of education, but my seven-year-old mind was too naïve to comprehend.

I can remember one incident in second grade in particular. My mother had gone to the annual "Parents Open House," a time for parents to go to school, look at student projects, meet with the teachers, and discuss their child's progress. When the parents arrived, they were asked to find their child's desk and be seated. After some searching, my mom found my desk at the front of the classroom, next to the teacher and far from all of the other students. Initially, she told me that she thought I must have been considered the smartest student in the class to have such an honored position in the front. However, she soon learned that my teacher put me there to keep me from talking to the other students and distracting the class.

Despite their disappointment in my performance at school, my parents kept encouraging me to concentrate. They would reward me not only for good grades academically, but also for behavior. In fact, I think that at least in the beginning, it was the behavior grades that my parents were concerned about more.

Every year, students take standardized aptitude tests. These tests are used to determine how well schools are educating their students and which top students should be placed in advanced classes. Throughout elementary school, I never performed well on these tests, and as a result, was not invited to participate in the honors classes. Although I did wonder whether I was smart enough to be included, I think my exclusion was more disappointing to my parents.

My father was determined to enroll me in the honors programs. He pleaded with the school to place me there. He pointed to my developmental milestones as evidence of my abilities, but the school was not convinced. They maintained that I was simply an above average student. Finally, my father convinced the school to have me take an IQ test. To everyone's surprise, with the exception my father, I performed well enough to be considered "exceptional." Using the results of this test as proof, my father beamed with confidence and started to push me harder and expect more. Soon the school changed its mind, and I was allowed to participate in honors classes.

Upon reflection, I think this event was pivotal to my success. Here is an example of where family support accomplished what individual talent could not. As a child, one's determination of self worth is largely based on what other people say. If you are constantly praised you tend to gain confidence, if you are criticized you can be devastated. In these most impressionable years, the messages parents give their children and the environment they provide can literally place a child on the road to success.

Say, for example, in my story my parents do not take an active role in lobbying for me to attend honors classes. Perhaps, I start to believe what the teachers say, that I am just above average. I do not associate myself with gifted individuals. Then maybe I lose confidence in my abilities and myself. These would be the experiences with which I would approach the remainder of life. Instead, my parents believed in my abilities even when I could not. Furthermore, they understood the importance of placing me in a challenging learning environment and were determined to find a way to have me included.

After attending honors classes, I made new friends, began to open my mind to new ways of thinking, and most important, considered myself capable and gifted. My parents through their support had provided me with the tools to build my dreams. And this has been my foundation.

Even though I had some academic difficulties in elementary school, I really enjoyed my childhood. I was eager to try all of the new experiences and opportunities that lay before me. Many young children are uncomfortable with unfamiliar situations and activities. Unsure of whether or not they will succeed, many youngsters prefer the security of routine. I think this is natural. However, at the same time children possess an insatiable curiosity. For children wrestling with these conflicting feelings, it is often up to the parents to provide encouragement.

My parents have always told me, "You never know until you try." Believing this motto, I seldom turned away from new opportunities and challenges. To me, it is better to have failed at trying something, than to not try, and constantly have the uncertainty of whether I would have succeeded had I tried. As a result, I discovered many new abilities and interests. In elementary school, I played violin, sang in church choir, acted in various school plays, participated in Cub Scouts, and played on multiple sports teams.

One of the four keys to success I mentioned is talent. Without having the ability to accomplish a goal, obviously you cannot succeed. Many people believe that talent is genetic, something you are born with, and you either possess it or you don't. I would argue that this is partially true. Although talent is largely genetic, when you are born, no one really tells you what your talents are. How do you know if you have been blessed with the genetics to become a great scientist, a world-class swimmer, or an acclaimed architect? Surely, there is an active process of uncovering hidden talents by being exposed to new situations. A potentially gifted artist will never know his or her talent unless given the opportunity to paint. In this regard, I think it is critical for parents to expose their children to as many different experiences as possible.

Furthermore, once these talents are revealed, it is just as important for parents to embrace and foster their diversity. In other words, I believe that different people are gifted with different talents, and no one talent is necessarily better than another. We have all witnessed parents pressure a child to succeed in an area that they are not able. Whether it's pushing them to play baseball or to become a physician, if the child lacks the ability or interest, the situation can become quite stressful for everyone. In fact, a child may lose self-confidence and self-esteem, not develop other talents, and never realize his or her true potential.

I believe I have been blessed with many different abilities, and thank my parents for helping me recognize and foster them all. During my elementary school years, many of the most important lessons I learned were not from books, but from my parents. Beginning in my youth, I knew that my parents supported and believed in me, and with this knowledge, I approached new challenges with both curiosity and confidence.

Once I was in middle school, I started to achieve academically. I am not sure if it was maturity, but for some reason, things started to click. At this age in school, there were many opportunities for academic contests, and being naturally competitive, I was eager to test the extent of my ability. For example, I remember several contests in math class. For one in particular, the teacher chose four of the best math students to represent the school, and to my surprise I was included. I participated in as many of these activities as possible. To me these contests not only challenged me to extend my abilities, but also instilled in me a sense of pride in academic achievement.

Then one day after hearing about a new academic team that was forming, I had an idea. As a child, I had often envied the relationship that other fathers had with their sons. Being blind, my father, although he supported me, was not able to play sports or participate in many of my scouting activities. Knowing that he would think I was talking about an athletic team, I went home that day and jokingly asked my father if he would be the coach of my team. He declined the offer. Later I told him that the team was an academic one called Future Problem Solving and described the nature of the competition. Immediately, he changed his mind and agreed to be the coach. Both of us were excited at the prospects of working together and participating in an activity where we both could excel. My father held weekly meetings after his work, and before long he led our team to the state level competition two years in a row.

My life continued smoothly as I gained momentum in both middle school and high school. To the delight of everyone, by the time I was a sophomore at Munster High, I had become quite accomplished. I was elected as a class officer, held the school record on the debate team, pole-vaulted in track, and ranked fourth academically in my class overall. Truly I had proven myself capable and felt comfortable with my new-found success.

At some point during my second year in high school, I learned about Phillips Exeter Academy and Phillips Academy, Andover, both college preparatory schools on the East Coast. I read about them in magazines and heard much from my father and was amazed at what I had learned. Gazing through pictures in catalogs, I imagined going to a school with talented students from all over the world, where I could take one of eight different foreign languages offered, while playing on one of their thirty different sports teams, or spending an evening watching stars at their observatory. I began to wonder if I could be accepted to attend such an institution. Again reverting to the "you never know until you try" mentality, I applied and was accepted. At first, I was overjoyed by my sense of accomplishment, but soon realized that I now faced a serious decision. Should I leave the comfort and security of friends, family, and past success or enter into a foreign environment and have to prove myself all over again? Considering both options, I decided that the opportunities and potential experiences outweighed the risks of leaving, and I enrolled at Exeter.

My adjustment to life at Exeter was not an easy one. In fact, after several semesters there, I was unsure whether I had made the correct decision to attend. I had earned average marks in class and no longer held the star status that I did at home. It was a difficult time for me. I was haunted by memories of elementary school and the thought of revisiting my struggle to overturn the label of "just average." Wondering whether this experience was worth the effort and monetary sacrifice, I also questioned my ability to succeed. For an adolescent trying to establish an identity, I think it's quite a shock to the system to go from one day being the top dog to having to start all over again. I phoned home on many occasions sharing my frustrations and doubts with my family. My parents listened and encouraged me to have faith in myself and continue moving forward.

Determination is a fundamental ingredient to success. Everyone at some point in their lives comes across challenges that seem insurmountable. What then? The question remains: Do you give up, or rise to the occasion? Throughout history there are many stories where humanity has accomplished amazing feats through will power. Consider, for example, the first climber to reach the top of Mount Everest, captured soldiers that endured through prison camps, or the survivors of cancer. All of these are powerful examples of what can happen with determination and the unwillingness to be defeated. For me, I have an example that is closer to my heart and that is the story of my father and his success despite innumerable odds.

My father was blinded at the age of sixteen. His parents and older sister had passed away leaving him the eldest of his two siblings. This occurred in Korea during a time where there was much discrimination against the blind and few opportunities for them to succeed. However, through his talent and desire, he became the first Korean blind person not only to attend college, but also to go abroad and to earn a Ph.D.

While feeling discouraged and doubtful during my time at Exeter, I recalled stories of his struggle, and began to draw strength from his example. Then I began to focus and adopted the mentality that failure was simply not an option. Determined to prove once again that in any circumstance or situation I was capable, I vowed to meet the challenges of Exeter. Soon I improved my grades and regained my self-confidence. My attitudes shifted, and instead of being intimidated by what people said I could not do, I welcomed the opportunity to prove them wrong. I soon realized some of these personal lessons learned at Exeter would serve me well, as I continued to excel and ultimately was accepted to Harvard University.

Attending Harvard was a thrilling experience. When I was in sixth grade, our family took a vacation to the East Coast, and while in Boston, we took a tour of Harvard University. At the time, I knew nothing about it's educational programs, philosophy, and facilities. All I heard from my parents was that this was "the best college in the world" and that was motivation enough for me to attend. While other kids my age hung banners of local colleges or universities with strong athletic programs on their bedroom walls, I proudly raised a Harvard pennant over my bed, determined to one day attend.

I am not sure if I can express the excitement that overcame me when I opened that acceptance letter. All of the hard work and effort suddenly seemed such a small sacrifice. However, my talent, family support, and determination did not accomplish this feat alone. I also had what I described as the fourth element of my success, luck. Statistics indicate that more high school valedictorians are rejected from Harvard each year, than there are spots. Clearly, no one can deny that these students have similar abilities and a strong will to succeed, so how do you decide who is accepted and who is rejected? I believe that ultimately some of the process comes down to chance.

Luck can mean different things to different people. To some it is just a random event, like winning the lottery it's a game of chance. To others luck may be perceived as a blessing in more of a spiritual sense. However, regardless of how you may define the term, most people can point to events in their lives that they consider to be lucky. If we believe that everyone has these random events, I believe the key question then becomes how do we react to these lucky circumstances? While it is true the initial lucky event itself we may have no control over, luck often leads to opportunity, and how we treat opportunity is what will determine success. History provides many interesting milestones attained largely through good fortune. Consider Alexander Fleming who discovered penicillin by accident, or Ben Franklin whose experiments with electricity were serendipitous. Now what would have happened if these individuals did not seize the opportunity that these lucky events provided and simply kept their discoveries to themselves? Our lives may have been dramatically different.

Here is why I consider my acceptance into Harvard partly lucky. As it turned out, my college counselor at Exeter, was a former admissions officer at Harvard University. How fortunate! However, this stroke of luck would not have accounted for much if I did not aggressively seek his counsel on what I needed to do to be accepted to Harvard. Every now and then life throws us a little pearl. We must not waste it. Remembering that luck is not entirely a passive state, we must use the opportunities it provides to tip the balance of life in our favor.

I really enjoyed my Harvard experience. Time spent there taught me that the world was far larger than my hometown of Munster, Indiana. I recall sitting at the dinner table with friends from Denmark, Seattle, and Korea and discussing philosophy and professional basketball in the same breath. Attending Harvard was both a great achievement and a humbling experience. It forced me to realize that success is a journey with temporary stops and not a final destination. Truly, my life was not going to be complete after graduating. There would always be more goals and challenges ahead.

At Harvard I began to view my life as a never-ending process of self-betterment. Throughout life you spend time accumulating experiences and knowledge. However, no one can know it all, and the more you learn, the more you realize the impossibility of uncovering all of life's secrets. It is important then to remember that it is not always how much you know, but how you face the unknown that will determine your success. In other words, while you may be proud of your accomplishments and your achievements, it should never be at the exclusion or expense of others.

Here is a story from my youth that I use as an example to illustrate my point, and coincidentally it was used as my admissions essay to Harvard University.

The room was a construction zone with LEGOS and matchbox cars arranged in a collage across the floor. My tower of blocks stood proudly in the corner of the room next to my coloring books. Today had been another busy day for me, but when my father turned out the lights, I was able to escape from the complexities of the world. Lying on my bed, I propped my five-year-old hands under my head. I stared into the darkness as the quiet of the night enveloped me. Soon the crisp sounds of tender hands turning the pages of a famil-

71

iar book broke the silence. I got settled into my bed, snuggling underneath my Sesame Street sheets. Moments later the warm and almost hypnotic voice of my father captured my attention. His words gently spoken took me far from the realm of kindergarten and into different lands, on some days accompanied by the "Tortoise and the Hare," and on others by the "Good Samaritan." My imagination ran free and was interrupted only once in a while by the gliding sounds of pages turning. Predictably, I fell into an untroubled sleep, only to awaken and long for the bedtime stories again.

One morning I studied my father's book that contained the roots of my now-vivid imagination. There were no pictures; raised dots filled the pages. I ran my fingers over the dots unable to imagine how my father could read from them. The strange thing about my discovery was that I had never considered my father blind. His blindness had never taken anything from our bedtime camaraderie. At nightfall he brought me into his world of wonderful darkness where my toys and my clothes couldn't distract us. My father, my imagination, and I were companions.

Now when I reflect upon my past, I think of how fortunate I was to have had a blind father who showed me how to see without eyes. Despite the fact that I have changed over the years, the effects of my father's bedtime readings are permanent. His readings allowed me not only to develop my mind and my creativity, but also has taught me a valuable lesson that I will never forget. Someone's worth cannot be determined by physical appraisal alone. Rather, we can learn something or receive insight from the most unusual people in the most unusual circumstances. Even though my blind father appears to be handicapped, to me he is more talented and capable than most of the people I know.

He has taught me lessons of life that I only could have learned through his perspective. Because of my father, I now view the world with a more open mind, willing to learn anything from anyone. Although I will never be able to read in the darkness, what my father was able to give me and continues to give me has helped clear my vision, fire my imagination, and see life as rich in opportunity.

After graduating from college, I attended the Indiana University School of Medicine and later finished my ophthalmology residency at the Duke University Eye Center.

Looking back, I truly feel blessed by the talent, family support, sense of will, and good fortune that has brought me to this point. It has been a long journey, but after thirty years my childhood dreams have come true, and much hard work and planning has come to fruition. Obviously, there are many other pivotal people and events in my life that have not been included in these pages but are equally important. However, the underlying theme remains the same. In order to succeed, you cannot be afraid to pursue your dreams. You must create opportunities and surround yourself with people who love and support you.

My life has presented me with a variety of challenges, many of which I am sure others can relate. I believe that my story is just an example of one way to travel down the road of success, and I look forward to what the future has in store.

by Paul. Kang M.D
Duke University Eye Center

Part III

7 Principles of Triumphant Life

Success comes in cans; failure comes in can'ts.
(Author Unknown)

I can do all things through him [Christ] who strengthens me.
(Philippians 4:13)

He will have to learn, I know,
    that all men are not just, all men are not true.
But teach him also that for every scoundrel there is a hero;
    that for every selfish politician, there is a dedicated leader.
Teach him for every enemy there is a friend,
    it will take time, I know.
But teach him if you can, that a dollar earned is far more value
    than five found.
Teach him to learn to lose, and also to enjoy winning.
Steer him away from envy, if you can.
Teach him the secret of quiet laughter.
Let him learn early that the bullies are the easiest to lick.
Teach him, if you can, the wonder of books.
But also give him quiet time to ponder the eternal mystery of birds
    in the sky, bees in the sun, and the flowers on a green hillside.
In the school, teach him it is far honorable to fail than to cheat,
Teach him to have faith in his own ideas,
      even if everyone tells him they are wrong.
Teach him to be gentle with gentle people, and tough with tough.
Try to give my son the strength not to follow the crowd
    when everyone is getting on the band wagon.
Teach him to listen to all men, but teach him also to filter all he
    he hears on a screen of truth, and take only the good
    that comes through.
Teach him if you can, how to laugh when he is sad.
Teach him there is no shame in tears.
Teach him to scoff at cynics and to beware of too much sweetness.

Teach him to sell his brawn and brain to the highest bidders
    but never to put a price tag on his heart and soul.
Teach him to close his ears to a howling mob
    and to stand and fight if he thinks he's right.

Treat him gently, but do not cuddle him,
  because only the test of fire makes fine steels.
Let him have to courage to be impatient,
  let him have the patience to be brave.
Teach him always to have sublime faith in himself,
  because then he will have sublime faith in mankind.
This is a big order, but see what you can do.
He is such a fine fellow my son.
            Abraham Lincoln's "Letter" to Teachers.

8.

Be a Positive Thinker Even in the Darkest Moment of Your Life

While they were saying, among themselves it could not be done, it was done. (Helen Keller)

Introduction

Many actors earned their fame while playing a superhero. Many series of supermen have come and gone, and some are still on television. But only in rare occasions do they become a true hero in real life. One of those few extraordinary human beings is Christopher Reeve who played "Superman."

Christopher Reeve always loved horses. He used to ride them everyday. In May of 1995, during the cross-country portion of a racing event in Culpeper, Virginia, Reeve's Throughbred, Eastern Express, balked at a rail jump, pitching him forward. Reeve's hands were tangled in the horse's bridle and he landed head first, fractur-

ing the uppermost vertebrae in his spine. Reeve was instantly para-
lyzed from the neck down and unable to breathe. Prompt medical
attention saved his life and delicate surgery stabilized the shattered
vertebrae and literally reattached Reeve's head to his spine.

After six months at Kessler Rehabilitation Institute in New Jersey,
Reeve returned to his home in Bedford, New York, where Dana, his
wife, had begun major renovations to accommodate his needs and
those of his electric wheelchair, which he operates by sipping or puff-
ing on a straw. Ironically, this most self-reliant and active of men was
now facing life almost completely immobilized and dependent on
others for his most basic needs. In addition, his condition puts him
at constant risk for related illnesses—pneumonia, infections, blood
clots, wounds that do not heal, and a dangerous condition involving
blood pressure known as autonomic disreflexia—all of which Reeve
would experience in the coming years.

In the years since then, Reeve has not only survived, but also has
fought for himself, for his family, and for the hundreds of thousands
of people with spinal-cord injuries in the United States and around
the world. He wrote *Still Me*, the heartbreaking, funny, courageous,
and hopeful story of his life. But, understandably he did not rise up
to occasion at first. When he woke up and found out that he could
not even breathe for himself, he wanted to die.

The major flaw in his plan was that he could not move. Even if he
really wanted to die, he had to ask someone to do it for him. While
laying in his bed, he thought about lots of things. He used to be a
superman. He had super powers. He used to rescue and help people
in need. Now, he could not lift a finger or wiggle his toes. What an
irony. Now he needs all the help in the world. He could not breathe
without a respirator. He could not chew and swallow food without
special help. He could not go to bathroom by himself. He thought
long and hard about the life that he had to live and concluded that
there is nothing left in his life.

The first person he met in the ICU, other than his doctors and
nurses was his mother. He told his mom what he thought. He begged
her to remove the life support from him. He told her that there is
nothing left in his life. In other words, he would rather die than go
on living. He couldn't find a reason why he had to stick around. His
mom agreed and decided to let him go. Now, the only person he had
to convince was his wife Dana.

When Dana walked into his room, he repeated what he told his mom. But she would not listen to him. She looked at him. She looked at her husband who was laying motionless. She could hear the respirator making noises. She could hear the heart monitor beeping. She looked at her husband and the uncountable tubes that were sticking in and out of his body. And she said, "You are still you!" Dana saved Christopher. More than that she inspired him to be what he is, a true hero. A true hero is an ordinary person who finds strength to persevere and endure in spite of overwhelming obstacles, just like our superman Christopher Reeve.

When Christopher was in the hospital, he received more than 35,000 letters and cards, encouraging him to fight, wishing him to get well. Prayers from many helped him. His friends helped him out. Of course, he could not have done anything without love and support from his family. But the one person who made him get out from the bottomless pit of self-pity and "live" was Christopher himself. Right after the accident, he thought he had lost himself. Things that defined him, being a dad, a husband, an actor, an active sports player, political activist were no longer there for him. But his wife landed him a helping hand, in the moment of darkness. It did not take too many words. It just took her one sentence to make him realize who he is. "You are still you." Whether sick or not, it did not make any difference. Being an actor, being a dad or being a husband—it is just part of who he is. He was still himself.

In the field of education, it is already a well-known fact that having self-respect is crucial to success. In order to respect oneself, one has to know who he or she is. That means having a positive view of oneself, valuing oneself worthy is a basis for educational success. It goes the same for life. When Dana and his children pleaded with Christopher to go on living, the first thing that came to his mind was, "Why should I go on living? What can I possibly do?" He thought long and hard and came up with a few reasons. He decided to continue to work as an actor. That was the craft that he worked with all his life. That he cannot walk or run did not really matter to him. He also wanted to give a voice to those who suffer from paralysis. Even though he was still lying in his bed breathing from respirator, he could see himself raising issues and helping fund spinal cord research as a political activist.

Since then, Christopher who cannot move, has not stopped moving. He has established a charitable foundation to raise awareness and money for research on spinal-cord injuries. Reeve's activism since becoming injured originally involved bringing more scientists into neurology to more quickly discover a cure, along with doubling the budget for the National Institutes of Health (NIH), a government agency in the executive branch that is part of the U.S. Department of Health and Human Services. His experiences with his own insurance company and, particularly, the experiences of other patients he had met at Kessler led him to push for legislation that would raise the limit on catastrophic injury health coverage from $1 million to $10 million.

Christopher accepted the positions of chairman of the American Paralysis Association and vice chairman of the National Organization on Disability. In partnership with philanthropist Joan Irvine Smith, he founded the Reeve-Irvine Research Center in California and he created the Christopher Reeve Foundation in 1996 to raise research money and provide grants to local agencies, which focus on quality of life for the disabled. Reeve's star power, along with marketing for research dollars, are reasons why spinal-cord injury research has been given greater attention and more money allocated to the cause.

Christopher Reeve is a true "hero." He did so many things for others. We praise him for his patience, persistence, endurance and all that. We clap our hands in great admiration because we know how hard he worked to overcome tremendous obstacles. But one of the most important reasons why we say he is an extraordinary human being is that he could see himself as a worthy human being when he was in the bottom of the darkest pit. When one is at the top, it is not hard to put a value in oneself. Generally, others put values for you, price tags such as your salaries, or nametags with your position on it. But it is totally different story when you fall down into the bottom. After loosing those titles and positions that once defined you, what would you become? What is the reason for your existence? What is your value? Would you still respect yourself as a vital and productive member of the society? But Christopher saw the misfortune as something that he could overcome in the end. He was able to see that his accident provided him with the unusual opportunity to serve others. It was possible because he saw himself as a worthy, respectable human being, even in the worst possible situation.

We don't know why misfortune happens and it doesn't matter. But "how" you accept the consequences or the results from those accidents does make difference. Christopher is living proof of it. Some learn more about themselves through hardship and difficulties. They learn to appreciate life and learn the greatness of human nature while overcoming such obstacles. Find your values. Find the reason for your existence. Find the ultimate goal and vision for your life. That will be your anchor when you are down.

When Christopher was interviewed by Barbara Walters, I waited with great anticipation for the interview for a long time. I was fascinated by his recovery, and I could identify myself with him in a way. After all, I jumped over a few hurdles of my own. Throughout his interview, all kinds of memories of my own came back. I could feel a huge ball of emotions bouncing all over the place. I remembered how I fought to regain my sight. I remembered the despair that I felt when I thought I had lost everything. I remembered why I wanted to kill myself. I remembered the joy that I felt for the first time. It was the day that I found myself, reason for my existence and purpose of my life. But mostly, I felt ashamed. Compared to his torments, my disability seemed like a minor injury. I could jump, and run if I wanted to. I could breathe without anybody helping me. I could hug and kiss my wife and kids anytime I wanted to. I could touch and feel. I could smell. But while I was down and blaming everything and everybody, Christopher Reeve was up and living. He knew what he wanted to do. He knew he is still himself.

I lost my sight when I was just a teenager. Having to go through puberty and an identity crisis is bad enough under the normal circumstances. But I pretty much lost everything I had, my sight, my dad, my mom, and at the end my sister too. I did not know who I was. I couldn't see anything except endless dark tunnels that I could not get out of. I thought God was punishing me for some reason that I did not know. I prayed and begged for a miracle. But it never happened.

Day after day, night after night, I was emerged in one thought. "Why?" First I wanted to know why I am getting punished. Second, I was trying to find a reason why I have to go on living. No matter how hard I tried, I could not find an answer. One day, I even tried to commit suicide. I told doctors and nurses that I could not get to sleep. I collected sleeping pills for a while, and then swallowed a handful of them. I did not see the point of living. What could I do? I was just a wretched human being who had nothing. My God had abandoned me. I was lost. Thankfully, my plan of ending my life did not succeed. It was not my stupidity that made me fail. It was a part of God's grand plan. In retrospect, it was not my time. God indeed had great plans for me.

Around that time, more than forty years ago, the Christian Broadcasting Network in Korea used to have a counseling program on radio. Callers from all over the country with all kinds of problems called to get help. I was one of them.

I waited anxiously. I had tons of questions to ask. I could hear my heart pumping faster and faster. Soon, I heard the familiar voice of Pastor Van over the phone. I was a long-time listener of that radio show.

"Thank you for calling us today. What can I do for you?"

I started to pour my little heart out. I told him how I lost my sight. How I lost my parents. I told him how I lost everything. And then, I asked him "why." I asked him why am I getting punished. Why God, who is supposed to be a loving God, who supposedly helps God's children in their time of need, refuses to help me. And I asked him why I have to go on living. It was a lot of questions; but I wanted to know; actually I needed to know. He waited until I finished. Then he introduced me to the scripture verses from 2 Corinthians 12:7-10

"But if I wish to boast, I will not be a fool, for I will be speaking the truth. But I refrain from it, so that no one may think better of me than what is seen in me or heard from, even considering the exceptional character of the revelations. Therefore, to keep me from being too elated, a thorn was given me in the flesh, a messenger of Satan to torment me, to keep me from being too elated. Three times I appealed to the Lord about this, that it would leave me, but he said to me, my grace is sufficient for you, for power is made perfect in weakness. So I will boast all the more gladly of my weaknesses, so that the power of Christ may dwell in me. That is why, for Christ's sake, I delight in weaknesses, in insults, in hardships, in persecutions, in difficulties. For when I am weak, then I am strong."

Finally, I saw the light at the end of the tunnel. I found someone with whom I can identify. I finally learned that my losses are not the punishment. God was not punishing Paul. God blessed him with so many other things instead. I finally learned why God did not fix my eyes. He had a grand plan for me. He took my sight to make me a greater tool. Yes, I found my purpose and reason for my humble existence.

Once I changed my outlook, everything around me changed drastically. When I was emerged in self-pity, when I was angry at everything, the world was very dark place. Every time I passed by a beggar, I thought, "Soon, I will be one of them" I thought that was the only thing that I could do. Being nothing. But, Pastor Van and Paul from the Bible taught me that I could be more. Once I learned that I have purpose and I have true value, I knew that God would use me to show his glory. That day, I knew I could become somebody. My disability became a tool. It was no longer a curse or a horrible punishment from God.

Now, these once useless eyes of mine are more powerful than I can ever have imagined. Because of them, I have met countless good friends. Because of them, I learned to appreciate so many things that others take for granted. Because of them, I could dedicate my life to serving others. Indeed, through my weaknesses, God showed his power and mercy.

As Christopher had his angel Dana to help him to realize who he is, I also had three angels who helped me find my way. Miss Sunhee Lee was one of many angels I met. She was a hospital social worker to the National Medical Center in Korea. I visited her and told her that I wanted to start a new life. She happily took me to the Rehabilitation Center for the Blind of Korea for a month and helped me to get basic training. She paid for the tuition for the first month, and she took me many places. She never felt sorry for me. She never felt ashamed to walk with me and to guide me. For the first time in my short life, I realized that there are people like Miss Lee who genuinely cares for a person like me. I felt loved and appreciated as a fellow human being. It was the first step to gaining back the self-respect that I forgot all about. Because of her, I learned that I have values. Because of her, I learn to respect myself. I learned from her that I am worthy.

Later I met another angel, Miss Soonkwi Kwon. She was a Girl Scout leader at one of the Quaker meetings. She initiated to raise a fund among members of her troop. That fund barely covered three months of living expenses, and when that fund was run out, Miss Kwon paid my tuition for a year out of her pocket. I am still in debt to her kindness, but I am most grateful to her for giving me a chance to meet my wife. I met my friend, my soul mate and my angel, my wife, through Miss Kwon. Through their love and support, through their encouragement, I realized one important fact, "I am important." Thanks to them I learned that I am worthy of self-respect.

What they thought of me also made a big difference. They were leaders of society who had graduated from prestigious colleges, and my wife was a college student at that time. Compared to them, I was nothing. I had nothing. But they never made me feel that way. They treated me as their equal, as the vital member of the society. It helped me tremendously. Because of them, I gained back my self-esteem.

We do not live in isolation. We are social beings. We interact with others constantly. This is why what others think of you is important. Some might argue that if you have strong self-esteem, you do not have to get assurances from others around you. But it is not true. Think of Christopher Reeve's case. What if his wife Dana agreed with him in the first place? What if she said, "I totally agree with you. I see what you are saying, I won't blame you for wanting to end your life." One thing is for sure; he would not be where he is right now. While some people are intellectually smarter than others, perspective and attitudes are learned behavior. It can be modified and controlled. When someone looses himself or herself in self-pity, when one loose his or her way, they always need someone to remind them who they are, what they can do.

Whether we recognize it or not, we learn new things everyday. We process new information and form our opinions accordingly. Our attitudes and our perspectives influence everything we do, including our learning process. It even affects how we view ourselves.

My two sons, Christopher and Paul, learned early on what disability is. We did not really have to tell them the differences between non-disabled people and disabled people. They absorbed everything from their mom and dad. Because of their mom, they learned to appreciate their dad as he is. They learned to respect me, and value me as a productive member of the society. Because of me, they learned that disability is not something to hide or be shamed. Through me, they learned that they could accomplish great things if they are willing to work hard for it.

It happened when Paul was just little kid. He used to say prayers before dinner. Everyday he recited the same prayer: "God is good, God is great, Let us thank for our food." But on one particular day, he surprised us with prayer of his own. He said: "Dear Lord, I wish I could have a seeing daddy. Give his sight back. So he can play baseball with me and drive for us, and he can teach me to ride a bicycle." In the educational point of view, his prayer showed both a positive and a negative attitude toward my disability. It had a positive aspect because his concern for me showed his compassion and empathy. He empathized with my disability and discomfort. He wanted to make me feel better. Compassion and empathy are the qualities that should be encouraged. It is crucial to nurture those qualities even when they are just little. I wanted to take that opportunity to do so. After the dinner, I sat down with Paul to talk about his prayers. I told Paul, "I lost my sight when I was little while playing soccer. Doctors did everything they could for me, but they still don't know how to fix my eyes. But, do you know what I think, Paul? I think maybe you can help them out when you grow up. I will wait till then." As soon as I finished my last sentence, I could hear Paul's excitement. He was so proud. His little heart was just about to burst with enthusiasm. He almost yelled out his promises, "Dad, I will become a doctor and then. And then, I will fix your eyes. You can play soccer, and play baseball, and do all kinds of stuff with me. Dad! You know what? I will also make you a car. I will make a car that even the blind can drive. Then we can go on a trip. Just the two of us."

More than twenty years later, his childhood dream came true. He became an ophthalmologist. He still cannot fix my eyes, but he is helping thousands of patients to see. It might seem like nothing at times, but a word of encouragement can change not just an attitude but also a life.

The negative attitude underlying Paul's prayer was how I cannot do what other "normal" people do, such as driving, playing baseball, or ride a bike. Nobody taught him what the blind can and cannot do, but he learned it by observing others around him. What Paul saw was the typical misconception.

In general, people tend to think disabled people are all alike. There is a stereotype that disabled people always need help or need to be looked after. Without even realizing it, non-disabled people put every disabled, blind, deaf, mute and others, in one huge basket and label them as inferior. Having a disability and lacking in ability are totally different things. There are many disabled people who function as productive members of society. And also there are many non-disabled who are just wasting their life, refusing to do better. These discriminatory attitudes to others should be corrected. I wanted to change how Paul saw "different" people. I wanted him to appreciate the differences of each individual. I wanted him to learn to respect them and accept them as who they are.

Around that time, I was working full time as a special education supervisor to the Northwest Indiana during the day. At night, I also taught classes at Northeastern Illinois University. My wife was also busy. She taught special education class full time. I guess my wife was lot busier than I was. She had to drive me around, and take care of our two sons. To run everything smoothly, everybody had to pitch in. While my wife washed dishes, I helped her out with kids. It was my job to give them a bath and tuck them in. Every night, I read them a book. It was our little ritual.

One night after we had dinner, I decide to give Paul and Chris a bath. We played around in the bathtub for a while, laughing and giggling. Soon, we heard my wife's footsteps; she was coming up to check on us. With a faint smile on her face, she reminded us that it was time for bed. I put towels around my two little rascals and headed to their bedroom. They changed into their pajamas and crawled into their beds. Paul and Chris were ready for their stories, but instead of telling them a story, I asked Paul a question.

"Paul, the other day you told God to fix my eyes so I can play catch with you and drive, right? You know, your mom can do that stuff much better than I ever can. But did you know? There is something that I can do better than anybody else. Guess what it is."

Paul thought long and hard but couldn't think of the right answer. Soon, he begged me for an answer.

"What is it? Come on! Dad! Please. What is it?"

I said to him, "Every night, I read you and Chris a bed-time story in the dark. It does not really make any difference for me, whether light is on or not. But your mom, well most parents can't read their kids a bedtime story when the light is not there. Isn't it great? I can read to you anytime, even when all the lights around the world are out."

I think Paul started to see a whole new world that night.

Fourteen years later, Paul was filling out applications for college. Quiet a few colleges asked for an essay, and Harvard was one of them. Paul had to write a short essay about the most significant event in his life. In his essay he wrote:

"His blindness had never taken anything from our bedtime camaraderie. At nightfall he brought me into his world of wonderful darkness where my toys and my clothes couldn't distract us. My father, my imagination, and I were companions. His reading not only allowed me to develop my mind and my creativity, but also taught me a valuable lesson that I will never forget. Someone's worth cannot be determined by physical appraisal alone. Rather, we can learn something or receive insight from the most unusual people in the most unusual circumstances. Even though my blind father appears to be handicapped, to me he is more talented and capable than most of the people I know. He has taught me lessons of life that I only could have learned through his perspective. Because of my father, I now view the world with a more open mind, willing to learn anything from anybody. Although I will never be able to read in the darkness, what my father was able to give me and continues to give me has helped clear my vision, fire my imagination, and see life as rich in opportunity."

The little chat that we had when he was just five years old changed him. It did not just change how he sees disabled people in general, but it also changed his perspective on life. It gave him the clear vision for his life. After getting an acceptance letter from Harvard, I got a phone call from the admissions office. The administration director said to me, "You must be very proud of your son. We need such a student like him who can see everything with positive view and attitudes." How you see the world around you, and how you see yourself does make a huge difference. It can determine your success or failure.

In the educational point of view, a student's attitude affects his or her academic success more than intelligence. Intelligence does matter, but perspective and attitude matter more than intelligence. Attitude and perspective can be learned and changed. But you do not have to be an educational psychologist to know the importance of it. We all experienced it, at least once in our lives. We also have seen how the perspective in the life of one person can change not just him or her but the entire nation in the examples of presidents Kennedy and Roosevelt. When you change the way you think, a whole new world opens up to you. Roosevelt found another world through his disability. He found new values in life, such as courage, faith, empathy, patience, and persistence. His perspective on life changed. While he needed help just to go to bathroom, he learned the value of every human being. As a result, he made every American to be able to enjoy " Freedom of speech. Freedom of worship. Freedom from want. Freedom from fear."

It does not matter how old your children are. You can teach them values and help them change their perspective on life. There is no such thing as "too late," in this kind of education. Through our own lives, we already experienced value and attitude changes. We might learn to listen to our parent's advice. We might go through dramatic changes such as getting married having children. We might read something from a book. Our values along with our attitudes change throughout our lives. Why? It is a part of our emotional development process rather than our intellectual development. But, we have to keep in mind that value education is most effective when a child is young. I do not have to tell you twice how hard it is to make teenagers do something, let along change their minds. But don't despair, it is not impossible; it's just hard.

There is an old saying, "what is learned in the cradle is carried to the tomb." It emphasizes the significance of the early education of values and behavior. One thing that you have to know as a parent is that you have to find the most effective way to educate your children. You have to know the intellectual level of your child. For example, if your child is seven years old (preoperational period), he or she is not capable to think logically. Therefore, read them a story they can relate to. This would be the most effective way to teach children that age a valuable lesson.

Second, you have to be a good role model. You can talk the talk, and read them a thousand books with great lessons, but if you do not model what you teach your children, all those efforts turn into nothing. Kids learn from their environment. They are like sponges and absorb everything around them. So don't forget to be a good role model for your children. It is the most effective way to etch great values on their minds for the rest of their lives. Don't wait for your children to grow up to talk about ethical issues. Do not assume it won't do them any good or they won't understand. They will understand. Read them books, talk to them, be a good role model for them. These will be the greatest investments you will ever have the privilege to make.

Finally, I would like to introduce the wisdom from the Bible. Colossians 3:21 sums up everything about self-esteem, pride, confidence, values, and attitudes. "Fathers, do not provoke your children, or they may lose their heart." This verse tells about how to educate our children. "Fathers, do not provoke." In other words, fathers have an important role to play in the lives of their children. Fathers' involvement is critical to a child's emotional development and educational process. Therefore, fathers should participate in every aspect of their children's life. When God created us in the image of God, God made men and women different. Basically, men and women are wired differently from the beginning. We think differently, talk differently. I don't mean that one is superior to the other. In an ideal world, it would be perfect if every child in America has the luxury of having both parents living together, but we still have to keep in mind the importance of father figures. Study after study proves that absent father influences the emotional wellbeing of children. It is time for fathers to take an active role in the lives of their children and to get involved. And the verse also tells us that we shall not irritate our children. "Do not provoke your children." We need to meet our children's needs. Children get mad when their needs are not met. In theory, human beings get mad when their needs are denied. Once our needs are met and our desires are fulfilled, we are content.

And the verse also tells us that we should not discourage our children. "They may lose their heart." Education is generally divided into three domains. They are: cognitive, affective, and psychomotor domains. It is essential to develop all three areas in balance; to be successful but affective domain is one of the most crucial parts that affect the development of a child. If one has high self-esteem and confidence, he or she can become a spectacular success even if he or she has average ability. It just shows the importance of encouragement.

Tell your children that you believe in them. Teach them to be proud of themselves. Teach them to love themselves. One word of encouragement goes long way. Remember, a positive perspective is learned behavior. We learn from our experiences. We learn it from others. Teach your child to see the brighter side of life. Help children to realize their values. You might forget what you said or what you did to encourage them, but they will remember. It will become their anchor whenever they are going through storms of their own life.

9.

Reach Your Full Potential
with Clear Vision

Everyone has inside of him a piece of good news. The good news is
that you don't know how great you can be! How much you can
love! What you can accomplish! And what your potential is!
(Ann Frank)

From time to time, people use "vision" as a synonym for a "sight." In part, the two words have similar meanings, but having a sight and having a vision is two different things. "Sight" is defined as an act or instance of seeing; state of being seen. The word "vision" contains the context of statesmanlike foresight, sagacity in planning. The word vision has a mental image that produced by imagination. You might have sight, but might not have a vision. In many cases, the opposite is also true, you might not have sight, like me, but you can have a vision for yourself.

Once someone asked Helen Keller what is the worst of all, being deaf or being blind? She answered that "the worst is having a sight but not having a vision. It is worse than never being able to see, or hear." She was right. When a person has a vision, he or she can see the future with clearer eyes. "To see is to get." If you want to be somebody, if you want to go somewhere in your life, first, you have to see it in your head. You have to know what you want to do in your life first. You have to have a vision to have a goal, plans, and strategies. This is why having a greater vision for oneself and for a society is one of the most common characteristics of great men and women in history.

If you go out and grab someone off the street and ask, who was the greatest civil-rights leader of this country, what would they answer? Better yet, who said the phrase "I have a dream?" Most Americans will be able to answer, "Martin Luther King Jr." without any problem. He was the youngest person ever to receive Nobel Peace Prize. His birthday is January 15. And on the following Monday after his birthday, we observe his birthday as a national holiday. Why do we still remember him? What made him such a great leader? The answer is simple. He had a vision. He had a vision for his country. Yes, he indeed had a dream.

Martin Luther King Jr. was born in Atlanta on the 15th of January 1929. As the grandson of the Rev. A.D. Williams, pastor of Ebenezer Baptist Church and a founder of Atlanta's National Association for the Advancement of Colored People (NAACP) chapter, and the son of Martin Luther King Sr., who succeeded Williams as Ebenezer's pastor, King's roots were in the African-American Baptist church. After going to local grammar and high schools, King enrolled in Morehouse College in Atlanta in 1944. He wasn't planning to enter the ministry, but then he met Benjamin Mays, a scholar whose manner and bearing convinced him that a religious career could be intellectually satisfying as well. After receiving his bachelor's degree in 1948, King attended Crozer Theological Seminary in Chester, Pa., winning the Plafker Award as the outstanding student of the graduating class, and the J. Lewis Crozer Fellowship as well. King completed the coursework at Boston University for his doctorate in 1953, and was granted the degree two years later upon completion of his dissertation.

Married by then, King returned south to become pastor of the Dexter Avenue Baptist Church in Montgomery, Ala. On the December 5th of 1955, after civil-rights activist Rosa Parks refused to comply with Montgomery's segregation policy on buses, black residents launched a bus boycott and elected King as the president of the newly formed Montgomery Improvement Association. The boycott continued throughout 1956 and King gained national prominence for his role in the campaign. In December 1956, the United States Supreme Court declared Alabama's segregation laws unconstitutional, and Montgomery buses were desegregated.

A national hero and a civil-rights figure of growing importance, King Jr. summoned together a number of black leaders in 1957 and laid the groundwork for the organization now known as the Southern Christian Leadership Conference (SCLC). King was elected as its president, and he soon began helping other communities organize their own protests against discrimination.

In the spring of 1963, Martin Luther King Jr. and the Southern Christian Leadership Conference led mass demonstrations in Birmingham, Alabama, where local white police officials were known for their violent opposition to integration. Clashes between unarmed black demonstrators and police armed with dogs and fire hoses generated newspaper headlines throughout the world. President Kennedy responded to the Birmingham protests by submitting broad civil-rights legislation to Congress, which led to the passage of the Civil Rights Act of 1964. Later that year King was a principal speaker at the historic March on Washington, where he delivered one of the most passionate addresses of his career. *Time* magazine designated him as its "Person of the Year" for 1963. A few months later he was named recipient of the 1964 Nobel Peace Prize. When he returned from Norway, where he had gone to accept the award, King took on new challenges. In Selma, Alabama., he led a voter-registration campaign that ended in the Selma-to-Montgomery Freedom March. King next brought his crusade to Chicago, where he launched programs to rehabilitate the slums and provide housing.

Many criticized Martin Luther King Jr. He was jailed. He was subjected to the same police brutality along with his fellow protestors. He had to fear for safety of his children and wife. He had to put forth every effort to keep his organization unified. Along with his fame and accolades as a great civil-rights leader came conflict within the movement's leadership. One of them was Malcolm X. His message of self-defense and black nationalism resonated more effectively with northern urban blacks than King's call for nonviolence. King also faced public criticism from "black power" proponent, Stokely

Carmichael. His efficacy was hindered not only by divisions among the black leadership circles, but also by the increasing resistance he encountered from national political leaders. J. Edgar Hoover, director of the FBI, launched extensive efforts to undermine King's leadership. These efforts were intensified during 1967 as urban racial violence escalated, and King's public criticism of U.S. intervention in the Vietnam War led to strained relations with President Lyndon Johnson's administration.

But criticisms and mountains of challenges did not stop him. Rather, he held his head up high and kept on going. In late 1967, King initiated a Poor People's Campaign designed to confront economic problems that had not been addressed by earlier civil-rights reforms. He called for a guaranteed family income. He wanted to focus national attention on the plight of the poor, unorganized workers of the city. The men were bargaining for basic union representation and long-overdue raises. What gave him such strength? It was his vision, vision for himself, vision for his kids and future generations, a vision for his people made him go stronger than ever.

But he never got back to his poverty plans. King lent his support to the Memphis sanitation workers' strike. On April 3rd of 1968, he showed a vision to his people. He showed a promise land. "We got some difficult days ahead," Martin Luther King Jr. told an overflowing crowd in Memphis, Tennessee, where the city's sanitation workers were striking. "But it really doesn't matter to me now, because I've been to the mountaintop." King explained, "I've seen the promised land. I may not get there with you. But I want you to know tonight, that we, as a people, will get to the Promised Land." The next day, April 4th, 1968, a rifle shot struck King as he stood on a balcony outside his second-floor room at the Lorraine Motel. Southern Christian Leadership Conference (SCLC) member Ralph Abernathy ran to the balcony and cradled his friend's head until the paramedics arrived and rushed him to St. Joseph's Hospital. Doctors pronounced King dead at 7:05 p.m.

Almost forty years later, his words still ring in the hearts of many Americans. His vision is still alive among us, inspires us, and moves us. But what if King had not had such a vision? What if he had given up on the way? What kind of society we would live in? Can you even imagine? Even today, we certainly have many social problems. We still have a long ways to go. We still have issues to take care of in social equality. I know, it is a lot of "what ifs," but I know one thing for sure, we are standing where we are, because of his vision and sacrifices.

Sometimes, people use words "vision" and "dream" inter-changeably. In many instances, it really does not matter. King's speech, "I have a dream" conveyed his vision perfectly. But these two words, dream and vision, have slightly different meanings. Vision is an end product of visualizing future goals and plans, therefore the clearer the vision, the better the dream. Dreams are an ideal, a fantasy, opposite of the reality itself.

Educators emphasize both "dream" and "vision." Having a vision and a great dream for oneself is vital to educational success. Educators, of course, whose studies are based on behavioral science, prefer measurable terms such as ambition and aspiration to vision or dreams. But the bottom line is the same. Whatever the term, light at the end of the tunnel, finish line, a goal, a vision is the most important factor that determines the academic success of a child.

One day, a first-grade teacher asked her class, "Which one is more important, the sun or the moon?" Everyone in the class had their favorites and had perfectly good reasons for their answers. One particular child said, "I think the moon is more important than the sun." The teacher asked him why and he said, "The moon comes out at night, when it is all dark. We can see things because the moon is there. But the sun comes out only during the day, when it is all bright and shiny. We don't need a light when it's bright, right? So the moon is more important than the sun." His answer brings a smile on our faces, because we all know how bright the sun shines. But, just like that first-grader said in his classroom, when it is dark, a little light seems a lot brighter. Vision is like a moon, it is like a little candle in the corner that brightens a whole room.

When we are in the darkest moment of our lives, when we want to give up, a vision makes us keep on going. Vision is like a light that is shining at the end of the dark tunnel. Whenever it gets darker, the light shines brighter. Because of that vision Christopher Reeve could keep on going. Because of that vision Martin Luther King Jr. could work harder in the time of hardship. Because of that vision, I could become what I am right now, the Honorable Dr. Kang.

However, we need to understand that vision is not just an issue of the moment of the darkness. One does not have to go through extreme circumstances to find the importance of vision. Clear vision is a guiding light in everybody's life. Whatever your goal, vision will help you get there.

My youngest son was just an ordinary boy. Because of his clear vision, he became an extraordinary man. His academic successes and his achievements are all credited to his vision, and careful planning to achieve the ultimate goal of his life. I remember Chris's graduation from the law school. On that day, I realized I have two great sons, Paul and Chris, standing right by my side. I have been proud of my sons all their lives. I am proud of who they were, who they have become, and I am sure I will be proud of who they will become later.

Right after the graduation, Chris started work for the Senate as a legislative assistant. Nine months later, Chris got a promotion. He became a council at the U.S. Senate Judiciary Committee for Senator Dick Durbin from Illinois. It was the talk of the Senate and of our hometown. There were several reasons for it. When you think of the lawyers, "gray haired gentlemen" comes to your mind. Especially, when you think of "council" to the Senate Committee, you tend to expect a lawyer who has tons of experience. You would never think to find a twenty-six-year old young man who just graduated from law school to wait for you in the office of the council to the Senate Judiciary Committee. It was the first unexpected surprise. And second, in general, you have to have at least two years of experience as a legislative assistant in the House of Representatives, before you move up to the Senate. Even after you move up to the Senate, you have to work hard for quite a long time as a legislative assistant to be promoted to a council. This was why Chris' promotion made such sensational news. He was way too young. He did not work in the House; instead he went to straight to the U.S. Senate right after graduating from Duke University Law School. On the top of that, he made a council in just nine months. It was possible because Chris had vision and followed through with his plans.

Just a month prior to his big promotion, an important event took place, which changed the dynamics of our father-son relationship. Chris always had a gift for writing. He was always writing something even before he went to grammar school. He did not just write for school newspapers. He was editor-in-chief most of the times. Because of it, I developed a habit of asking Chris to proofread most of my important letters or speeches. Soon he became my best assistant. For more than fifteen years, he was my personal secretary, speechwriter, research assistant, editor, and more.

But a lot had to be changed after his graduation from law school. He got a new job. At first I did not want to bother him that much, after all, I know what it is like to have a brand new job. It could get a little crazy. On the top of that, he was planning his wedding. I understood how hectic his schedule could be, so I waited and waited. I thought I would get a better chance once Chris had some time to settle in his new job. It did not get any better. Then I said to myself, "After the wedding, everything will be back to normal. We will find some time to work on our stuff, together." But, everything stayed the same. Chris was still busy and had no time for me. He always had to work late, and had to go to office even on weekends. I did not want to nag him, after all, I am a very understanding father, right? But after a few months of waiting, I was just about to explode with frustration. Every time I called Chris, he told me he was too busy to help me out. Obviously, I got frustrated. Every time Chris told me that he had to work late, I got a little bit more frustrated, and at the end, I could not take it anymore. One day, I finally snapped.

I asked him with sarcasm, "Is it because you are incompetent, that takes you longer than others to finish your job?"

Chris did not say anything, but the next day I received a fax from him instead. He wrote;

Dear Dad:

You have insulted me this morning by saying that I am incompetent. You did not know what I am doing. I am working very hard to get promoted to be a council this August. I have been sharing responsibilities of the council who is leaving his office in August. I want you to respect me, and what I am doing.

Chris.

I called him right away and apologized. I also told him how proud I was to be his father. In my frustration, for a moment, I forgot how focused Chris was. He always had clear vision and knew how to go about his life, and where he wants to be. If you want to succeed, have a clear vision. Chris's promotion was not a lucky coincidence. He knew there would be a council position opening in eight months. That was why he was working day and night. He was like that even when he was in law school. In order to secure his position in the

Senate after graduation, he had a fellowship at the office of Senator Edward Kennedy. He never had a decent break over the summer, but his hard work is getting rewarded right now. Clear vision will help you to find a way around life. When your vision gets clearer, it gets easier to develop the necessary abilities and talents.

Over thirty years ago, I came to America with nothing but a dream for myself and for my family. Four years later, in 1976 Chris was born. That same year, I received my Ph.D.

Think for a moment and go back to the time Chris was born. At that time, my relationship with Chris was very simple. He was a newborn. He knew nothing, being so fragile and vulnerable. For a while, I was always at the giving end of things, and Chris was mostly at the receiving end. Through the ups and downs of twenty-six years, our relationship went through many changes. It was a slow process, hardly ever noticeable. But the end result is shockingly wonderful. Look at us right now. Now, I am not always standing in the giving end. And Chris is hardly ever standing in the receiving end of things anymore. Even though I have lot more life experience than Chris, now we are standing with each other, shoulder to shoulder as equals. As vital members of the society, and as fellow human beings who are striving for excellence and higher achievements, we help each other out. If Chris never had a clear vision for his future, we might never have had this wonderful spirit of camaraderie.

When Chris was in 5th grade, he received a homework assignment from one of his language-art classes. It was more of humongous project than a simple assignment that a child could do in an hour or two. His homework was to write an autobiography as a sixty-five-year old retired man. Before the assignment, he always thought that he would go to Stanford and become a scientist. He did not have specific plan. It was just a vague idea that was roaming around inside of him. But, as his research progressed, his dream started to shift.

In order to get a clear blueprint of your life, you have to look into every detail. First, you have to look into yourself and find a vision for yourself. You have to look ahead, ten years, twenty years, maybe thirty years, and more. You have to decide your ultimate goal. What do you want to achieve? What do you want to do with your life? I know, it is overwhelming process, and can look impossible, but once you get this far, everything will start to fall into place. With a clear vision, you will find you process goals with ease. Process goal are steps you have to take in order to reach your ultimate goal. For example, getting a good grade in high school to go to college is a short-term process goal for middle-school students. And attending college to get a good job will be a long-term process goal. The last thing you need to do is make plans and develop strategies and behave objectively, such as doing your homework and etc., to achieve those goals. It looks overwhelming and complicated. Well, it indeed is a long and complicated process. It might be one of the hardest tasks one might have to do. But like Henry Kissinger once said, we need a purpose and direction to be somebody and go somewhere. He used to say to younger generations that without a clear direction, you will go nowhere.

While writing his autobiography, Chris found his goal. Instead of becoming a scientist, he decided to retire as a U.S. Supreme Court Justice. He wanted to help others in need. His vision was to make a difference in society. He wanted to become a Supreme Court judge and promote social justice. That was his long-term goal. Page after page, he wrote down the steps that he had to take to become what he wanted to be. In order to become a Supreme Court Justice, he had to become a judge first. To become a judge, he had to become a lawyer. In order to become a lawyer, he had to go to the law school. And before that, he had to go to college. In his little book, he had plans for everything. He even wrote about how he was going to meet his wife in detail.

As he grew up, his book changed a little. He went to the Wilbur Wright Middle School, and went on to Andover. But instead going to Princeton, he went to the University of Chicago. Instead of the Harvard Law School, he decided to study at the Duke Law School. He had to adjust his path because he learned that he could not control everything. But his vision always guided him through his life's journey.

Nowadays, I see many young people wasting their lives. They wander aimlessly. They are not stupid; some are very intelligent people. Some even graduated from prestigious colleges. Getting a degree from a good school does not guarantee your success. It might help, but it is not a guarantee. Do you want to know why so many people fail? They do not have a vision. In most cases, they just have process goals. Their goal was getting into a good college, maybe becoming a doctor or a lawyer. But once they got into a great college, and became a doctor, they don't know what to do. Their goal just disappeared. Where do they go from there? What do they have to do next?

There are many benefits for having a vision. It gives you a clear direction in your life. It ensures greater success in many ways, academically, financially, etc. It gives you strength in time of need. But there is another benefit that comes with having a vision. It is not as obvious as others, but it is a definite benefit. Having a vision gives you opportunities to develop your true talents. Most of the time, we do not know our true potential. Mostly it is because we generally do not have a chance to develop our talents, but having a vision gives you more chances than you can ever imagine.

People with a goal develop their abilities with ease. There are many reasons why. There are three ways to find out what your natural abilities are. The first method is the standardized mental testing approach such as intelligence tests. You take series of tests to measure your intelligence, creativity, and aptitude. The second method is the job analysis approach. You compare your functional abilities with your knowledge and skills. The third method is the situational approach. It is putting yourself in an actual situation and finding out ways if you have a talent for it or not. But, if you have clear goal, you start to use the situational approach to develop your abilities. People with goals can do their best in situational approach. Whenever they are in the situation, instead of giving up they will find a way to work it out. It is because they know they have greater things to do. It is because they have a guiding light shining in front of them in the moment of uncertainty. Overcoming the difficulty, developing a new talent and ability becomes a behavior objective for those who have long-term goals and vision.

This is the eighth book I've written. So far, they have been great successes. But, until I wrote my first book, I did not know I could write. I only had a one goal in my mind. I wanted to show God's wonders and glory through my weakness. I started to write a little bit about my life each day, and soon it became a book. Because I had a goal, even though it was just a simple one, I was able to find and develop a new talent. My book was a tool that connected me to so many great people around the world, such as the Bush family. Because of my book, I could do much more for the disabled around the world. Yes, it was possible because I had a goal. Sometimes, you don't know what you can do until you are forced to do it.

When I proposed to my wife, I gave her a new name. "Suk Eun Ok," which means "stone, silver, and jade." Each letter represents a period of our life together. The jade period was the "giving back" period. My wife and I decided to give back what we had received. We wanted to show God's glory and mercy through us. I thought writing a book about it would be a great idea. I wanted to tell people how God changed me and used me to do his work.

The last year of the jade period was 1992, the same year the Rotary International Foundation celebrated its 75th anniversary. I was asked to speak at that convention. I did not know I could move people with my words until I opened my mouth in the convention. Till then, I never knew my words carried such power. I was standing in the middle of the huge convention hall. I thought I was shaking a little with great anticipation, but it might have been excitement. Finally, I opened my mouth and started my speech, "People Who Make the World a Better Place."

As soon I finished my speech, I could hear people start clapping. It grew louder and louder. Soon I realized that I was getting a standing ovation from thirty thousand leaders from 158 nations. My heavy Korean accent did not matter. Because I had a vision, I got a chance to find my true talents and develop it thoroughly.

By now, you can see how important it is to have a great vision. Having a great vision, a great dream is important, but it does not ensure 100 percent success. In order to lead a successful life, you have to have more than a great vision. You need to have a great support system. That is the people who will encourage you when you are down. You also need to evaluate yourself. You need to know where to devise a strategy, modify your goals and action plans. There are two different ways to evaluate your accomplishments. One is a relative evaluation, which is known as a norm-referenced evaluation. The other is an absolute evaluation, which is also known as a criterion-referenced evaluation.

Here is an example of the relative evaluation system. Quiet while ago, I had a chance to visit a long-time friend of mine. After dinner, we talked about our good old days in college. In the midst of it, his son ran into the living room. I could not see his face, but I could tell it from his voice that he had great news to tell. His voice was full of excitement and pride.

"Mom! Mom! Come here! I have something to show you."

"What is it?"

"Come on, Mom! You have to see this. See."

He was holding onto one of the math tests that he'd taken a day ago.

"I got 100 percent. I got an A. I got an A."

Now, he was singing his grade. But his Mom calmly asked him a question.

"What did your friend Matt get?"

All the excitement and happiness disappeared instantly and somewhat grumpily he answered to his mom.

"He also got a hundred."

"Hmmm. I guess test must have been easy."

The relative-evaluation system compares the accomplishments of one person against another. Instead of celebrating their achievements, such as getting an A on exam or scoring a goal in the soccer game, we always want to know how others are doing. On the other hand, the absolute evaluation measures your accomplishment against the goal. If the goal of your child was to get a B on the math test, and he or she gets it, he or she deserves a pat on his or her shoulder, a smile, and words of encouragement, "great job."

There are many advantages and disadvantages for each scoring system. In school, we tend to use both systems to offset any disadvantages one particular system can cause. Problem is, life is not a simple test. Life is more like a marathon. Life has a goal that one needs to reach. And you have to keep on running until you reach that finish line. This is one of the reasons why the relative-evaluation system tends to loose its attractiveness. Of course, it is important to run faster than others, but people say a marathon is a fight against oneself. Life is also a fight against oneself. It is important to jump higher, run faster, learn more, and possess more than others. But that is not the end. In order to reach your goal, you have to beat the greatest opponent, yourself.

When you start to compare yourself with others, there will always be a winner and a loser. It would be great if you can always be a winner, but that is not always the case. There will always be someone who runs faster than you. There will always be someone who has better things or know more than you. Whenever you compare yourself to others and loose, you get discouraged and shamed. Basically, you feel like a loser, second-grade citizen. It is a harsh reality, even for adults. But for children, its affects can be magnified. Constant exposure to such pressure will cost them their self-esteem. They will lose respect for themselves. Soon they will value themselves to be nothing.

On the other hand, the absolute evaluation system does not create such problems. We know we are all unique individuals. We look different, even the twins do not look exactly the same. When we are born, we are all blessed with different talents. One's gift is different from others. You might be able to throw a ball across the football field without a problem, and I might not be able to do the same. But instead, I can run faster than anybody. How can you possibly compare such different talents? It is like comparing apples and oranges. It is pointless.

In absolute evaluation, we compare ourselves against our goal. Instead of counting how many people are running in front of me, or behind me. Absolute evaluation measures how far I have come. The ultimate goal is to finish a race. Whether I am the first one to cross the finish line or last one to do so does not really make a difference. Finishing a long journey itself is a great achievement. Absolute evaluation indeed helps out children more in many aspects. They feel more accomplished. They are goal oriented and they are willing to help each other out to achieve the same goal.

You need to find out your abilities and talents. Finding your true talents is vital to your success. Even if two individuals who have the exact same vision for their future, such as making the world a better place for the future generation, depend on their abilities and talents. And processing goals would be different. It is like going to New York. The destination for New York is the same, but there are hundreds of means to get there. You have to know your strengths and weaknesses.

Don't just use your eyes to see. "To see is to get." You have to see the world with vision. Find out what you would like to do and what you are good at. Develop those talents. Later, you will be able to contribute your unique gift to society. Do not compare yourself to others. You are different from others. What is the point in wasting your precious time comparing yourselves to others? Just look ahead. Look at your finishing line and goal.

Life is a journey into your vision. See how far you came alone. Whenever you feel like you are a failure, whenever you feel despair, remember those people who overcame many obstacles before you, Martin Luther King, Christopher Reeve, and Helen Keller. And just move ahead. Never forget to look for that little light shining brightly in the darkest corner. Yes, never forget why you are running. Never lose your vision.

10.

Develop Serving Leadership by Giving the Best You Have to the World

As the army of compassion, together we can do.
(President George W. Bush)

Almost all noble attributes—love, faith, loyalty, and courage could be transmuted into ruthlessness. But, compassion alone can stand apart from the continued traffic of good and evil. Compassion is anti-toxin of the soul. *(Eric Hoffer)*

I guess it was about a month after the 9/11 terrorist attacks. The nation was still in shock. The United States government was trying its best to heal the nation as soon as possible. In an effort to do so, President Bush came on television for a press conference, the first one since the attacks. Americans wanted to know how things are progressing and some sort of assurance that everything will be fine. Americans wanted to hear that from the leaders of the government. First, President Bush assured the nation with clear pictures. He answered many questions, but for some of them he did not have answers to give.

After answering countless questions from reporters, President Bush addressed the children in America. He asked children to raise funds by washing cars or mowing lawns. And he asked every child in America to send a dollar donation to the White House. He promised them he would use that money to help the starving children in Afghanistan. He told them the fact that one out of three children in Afghanistan have lost their parents and are suffering. He assured them that they will get returned more than a dollar. He said that they would become tomorrow's compassionate leaders.

The next day, many praised him for instilling an important value, compassion, to youth in America. This project not only took American children's mind off of horrible terrorist's acts, but it also gave each child an opportunity of something to do. The president's project taught them the value of the compassion.

As an educator, I supported President Bush's charitable project. And I was even compelled to write a short letter to him.

In my letter, I said:

"I strongly support your charitable and educational project to teach sixteen million school children compassion, which is an integral part of service and leadership. I am enclosing a check of one thousand dollars for your project, which I got as an honorarium from McCormick Theological Seminary. Your father once said that teaching compassion at home is more important than what the president does at the White House. In my speeches or lectures for younger generations; I used to quote your father, now I am excited to quote you as well."

There are many ways to measure one's success. Someone might say that the assets one accumulates during his or her lifetime measures his or her success. Someone might say that the awards and achievements one accomplishes are a fair measure of success. But, really, what are the most important qualities of a great person? Why do we admire and respect certain people while we despise others who achieve so much and build such wealth for themselves? Being successful is not always equal to being a great person. Many use these two terms interchangeably. But, when you look into it, the differences are clear.

The simplest example can be found in the Bible, Luke's Chapter 10:25-37. In this parable, a man was going down from Jerusalem to Jericho. On his way to Jericho, he fell into the hands of robbers. They stripped him of his clothes, beat him and left him to die. Soon after, a priest passed by him. Likewise, When a Levite came to the place and saw him, passed by on the other side. The beaten man was glad, even in the midst of his miserable pains, he was sure the priest or Levite would help him out. But an unknown Samaritan helped the beaten man.

When we think of a "great" person, we have a tendency to imagine powerful political figures, business tycoons, Nobel Prize winners, or someone cited in a history book. In many ways, they are all great people. But you don't have to be in a powerful position or have thousands of dollars to change the world. You do not always have to have many college degrees to become a great person. Sometimes, little people like you and me can write history. Yes, it indeed happens and still happens everyday.

In Washington, D.C., there are four memorials in honor of the former presidents: George Washington who was the first president; Thomas Jefferson who wrote the Declaration of the Independence; Abraham Lincoln who freed the slaves, and Franklin Roosevelt who led World War II victory and saved the nation from the Great Depression.

And recently, all of us finally got a chance to say thanks to those Americans who built their dreams into great movements that helped people across America and the world. On February 13, 2002, the Points of Light Foundation unveiled Extra Mile Pathway. This new national monument honors a number of America's private citizens who dedicated their lives to creating solutions to serious social problems.

The first bronze features Reverend Edgar J. Helms, the founder of Goodwill Industries. It is not a building like other memorials, but a mile-long path. More than seventy hand-sculpted bronze medallions form The Extra Mile Volunteer Pathway, a one-mile path adjacent to the White House and U.S. Treasury Department. Each medallion measures forty-two inches in diameter and features a rendering of the honoree, a description of his or her accomplishments, and a quotation. There are four persons in the first of honorees. Clara Barton who founded the American Red Cross, Martin Luther King Jr. who is the one of the greatest civil-rights leaders, Susan B. Anthony who pioneered the women's movement, and Edgar J. Helms who founded Goodwill Industries. These four persons gave their lives to make this world a better place to live instead of accumulating their own wealth.

Let us look into the first bronze feature, Reverend Edgar J. Helms, the founder of Goodwill Industries who reached out to thousands of people who were unemployed and helped them gain the dignity of economic independence.

Edgar James Helms was born on January 19, 1863, in a lumber camp near the wilderness town of Malone, New York, just south of the Canadian border. His father, William Helms, was a logging crew superintendent and his mother, Lerona, was a camp cook. In 1865, taking advantage of the 1862 Homestead Act, the family moved to Nashua, Iowa. In 1878, at age fifteen, Edgar Helms became a printer's apprentice at the *Beacon*, the local newspaper, thus beginning what he hoped would be a career in journalism. Helms reluctantly left the *Beacon* three years later to attend Cornell College, a staunchly Methodist institution in Mount Vernon, Iowa.

Because of his limited funds, Helms worked numerous hours in addition to his studies, making college life difficult. Helms left college in the spring term and within six months embarked again on a newspaper career. He led a successful county campaign to unseat "a rum candidate for legislature." Although Helms was unsuccessful in his bid in public office, his experiences ultimately led him back to Cornell and into a life as a minister and a missionary. He sold both his Peterson Patriot and Sioux Rapids newspapers and used these funds to support his final year in Cornell and later at the Theological School of Boston University.

At the age of thirty-two, Helms was offered the ministry post at Morgan Chapel in Boston's South End. Here, at a dilapidated inner city mission is where Helm's vision of Goodwill began. From the outset of his work at Morgan, Helms was focused on using the church to meet community needs. Under Helm's supervision, the Chapel provided bathing and laundry services, created a children's center, a nursery, kindergarten, and led the effort against local prostitution and underworld criminal elements in its parish. In the fall of 1896, Helms added an industrial school and night school, and in 1897 added a music school. In 1899, his wife Jean, after tending to others with tuberculosis, contracted the disease herself and died later that year.

But his work did not stop there. Helms kept on going with his work. The 1902-1903 financial collapse created widespread unemployment among the poor of his area and reduced the already poor population to be even more destitute and many of the middle class to borderline poverty. For a time, Helms was able to support these people by seeking donations from the more affluent sections of Boston, however this method of fund-raising was not sustainable.

In 1902, Helms took a burlap sack to these same sections of Boston and asked for cast-off shoes, clothing, and virtually anything he could carry away. He put men and women of the South End to work repairing the collected items, which were then sold for modest amounts. Helms noted that the poor retained a large measure of their self-respect and dignity if they were required to pay, even a token amount, for whatever was offered them. This approach became the Goodwill Store concept.

By 1905, the relief work, now bringing collected goods by horse-drawn wagons, had grown to such a volume that Helms incorporated these efforts into an organization known as the "Morgan Memorial Cooperative Industries and Stores, Inc." These stores were run as a nonprofit, charitable corporation. The corporation operated not only in his church building but also expanded into several adjacent houses.

With Helms as the driving force, Goodwill Industries gradually spread across the United States, offering programs to help the "unemployables" enter the work force. By 1926, Helms was touring the world telling the story of Goodwill Industries and laying the groundwork for an international movement. When the Great Depression produced mass unemployment, Goodwill Industries narrowed the focus of its services to people with disabilities.

Helm's vision set an early course for what is now a billion dollar nonprofit organization. Today, Goodwill Industries International is one of the world's largest private-sector employer of people with disabilities and disadvantaged conditions. Helm's concept of providing "a chance and not charity" has expanded into 187 autonomous members in the United States and Canada, and fifty-four associate members in thirty-seven countries outside of North America. His energy has helped thousands recognize and fill their individual roles in society and the workplace.

Great people are not just successful, but adored and respected by many even decades after they are gone. It is because of their leadership and service based on their compassion. Helm's project first started because he felt the pain and suffering of others. It is so important to have compassion. Without compassion, one cannot fathom to serve others. Without compassion, there is no leader. Without compassion, we are nothing.

Webster's dictionary defines compassion as "suffering with another." Compassion is a sensation of sorrow that is excited by the distress or misfortune of another. It is a knot in your stomach when you see a starving child. It is an urge you get when you see a sick child. Poet Eric Hoffer said that compassion alone stands apart from the continuous traffic between good and evil. He also said that compassion is the "antitoxin of the soul": where there is compassion even the most poisonous impulses remain relatively harmless.

Compassion is a universal value that should be taught and instilled in children to ensure their success in life. The former President Bush used to emphasize the importance of having compassion. He said, "teaching compassion is more important than what the president does at the White House." It is especially true for those who have to lead others. Imagine, what if we have a leader who did not have compassion? How would he know what people need? Would he know the suffering of his people? Compassion teaches vital values that must be learned early on in a child's life.

Even though compassion is the basis of the great leadership, without willingness to do something, compassion loses its values. Willingness to serve others, which is the basis of compassion, is an action plan. Let's go back to Edgar Helms. What if he did not have a will to serve others? He could not have started the Goodwill Industries. This is the difference between great people and ordinary people. In some degrees, everybody feels compassion. Sometimes we shed tears because we can feel the pain of others. But, how many of us actually do something to help them out? Not many. This is why we praise people who actually get up and do something. This is why we have the Extra Mile Pathway.

Some argue that a person is born with a character trait such as compassion. But arguably, character can be built, and improved with proper guidance. A few years after loosing my sight, I met my wife. She dedicated her life to help me. She sacrificed so much without ever asking anything in return. Her compassion and spirit of giving was the light that guided me through the roughest part of my life. Maybe, my children Paul and Chris got their spirits from their mother. But it is an absolute truth that their education played a major role in building their characters.

I can witness to the point of building characters. My second son Paul transferred to Phillips Exeter Academy after completing his sophomore year in Munster High School and Chris attended Philips Academy Andover after his graduation from the Wilbur Wright Middle School. Of course, they were great kids even before they attend those great schools. They were compassionate and always willing to help others. But what Phillips Academy did was they gave a clearer vision; they instilled the spirit of service and leadership in core of their vision.

Education Weekly named Andover and Exeter as one of the most prestigious schools in the United States. For more than 200 years, Phillips Academy has withstood the test of time. Despite wars fought on American soil and afar, economic depressions, and social upheavals, the two schools have managed to merge into the 21st century as one of the most prestigious schools in the nation.

Both school have an impressive list of alumni, including Samuel F.B. Morse, originator of the Morse Code; former President George Bush; current President George W. Bush and his brother John "JEB" Bush, the governor of Florida; actors Humphrey Bogart and Jack Lemmon; Tarzan author Edgar Rice Burroughs and Pulitzer Prize-winning author Tracy Kidder; and a slew of acclaimed scientists, politicians, journalists, businessmen, and artists. According to recent research, one out of every thirty-five graduates from Phillips Academy is in the *Who's Who of America*. Also, the probability of its graduates becoming millionaires is highest in nation. Why is that? How did they manage to provide society with great leaders for more than two hundred years? What is their secret?

Of course, both schools have a rigorous selective process. Selecting quality students might be the reason for their success, but it is more than that. There are many factors that contribute to their success; a solid academic program, a successful philanthropy program, and a commitment to help students succeed in the classroom and beyond are few ingredients for their educational success. But, educators around the world find the Phillips Academies' commitment to building character is the most important factor that makes the difference.

Their school motto is "Non Sibi." It is Latin, which means "Not for self." It has been taken from the poet Lucan's Pharsalia, in a line saying that Cato was born not for self but for the entire world. The message was consistent with the principles of the founders of Phillips Academy. In other words, it is our responsibility to give back. Their philosophy, "not for self" is embedded in everything they do from the classroom to after-school activities. Even though the role of Christian religion in the school has started to fade, it still influences each student in many ways. Both schools still have worship services every Sunday morning. Every student who attends Phillips Academy also has to take at least two religion classes to graduate. Their effort in building character does not stop in the classroom. Each student is encouraged to do volunteer work around the community throughout his high school years.

I am proud of Chris who grew up to be a compassionate leader. He always worked hard and got good grades. He worked hard on the school newspaper and played many sports. During his senior year, Chris took on more roles as a compassionate leader. He cofounded a newspaper. He started to do more volunteer work. As a worried father, from time to time, I scolded him for spending too much time on volunteer work.

"Who will remember your service? Who cares what you have done for them? You just missed out on a chance to get a great education for nothing." He answered, "People in the nursing home will remember. I worked my butt off to sell T-shirt, which I designed. I managed to collect fifteen hundred dollars for that nursing home. And every time they turn on the TV, they will remember."

I was speechless. I am the one who experienced the compassion of others firsthand. I am the one who knows the importance of serving others. I am the one who decided to give back. But, I still had more to learn from my son. While, my actions, serving others is the end result of conscious decision-making process, the philosophy of the Phillips Academy, "not for self" was embedded in everything Chris does. Even though, he was just a high school student, he was already living for others. He was already serving others, making a difference.

Chris attended the University of Chicago. The University of Chicago is famous for many Nobel Prize winners from various fields. Also, it is famous for its rigorous curriculum. But Chris bloomed and flourished at the University of Chicago with ease. He managed his time efficiently. He managed to double major in public policy and economics.

While he was at the University of Chicago, his effort to serve others and make the world a better place did not stop. He established the university community service center for needy. When he was a junior, he ran and was elected as the student liaison to the University Board of Trustees. Because of his active volunteer work and leadership, he received Tomorrow's Leader Today Award, which is given to young leaders who are under thirty years old. Also, when he graduated, he received the Howel Murray Award from the University of Chicago Alumni Association for his leadership and services.

His leadership and activities played a major role when he applied for law school. He had developed the leadership qualities for serving others that every law school looks for in its applicants. While doing volunteer work, and trying to make a difference around him, he had chances to meet great people who provided him with great recommendations. On the top of everything, because of his willingness to serve others, he had a chance to meet the love of his life, Elizabeth. Even after he went to law school, he put every effort to serve others. Now he makes a difference everyday as a council at the U.S. Senate Judiciary Committee.

Great leaders don't rule over people. Great leaders are compassionate. He or she hears the pain of his or her people. They suffer with them. A great leader does not abuse his or her powers. They are there to serve. Once former President Bush said that the most important aspect of character that great a leader must have is compassion. He also said that the most important job a leader has to do is to serve.

You do not have to send your children to prep school to build their character. It should start at home. Former President Bush once said that he learned to be a compassionate leader at home. He learned the value of serving others from his mother. When he was little he wanted to have his own room. He was sick and tired of sharing everything with his brother. But, his mother refused to do so. She told him that if he cannot even understand and be compassionate to his own brother's need, how could he possibly understand others and serve them?

What he learned from his mother, when he was a small child, stayed with him, and he passed it on to his son. His son, President Bush, is a compassionate leader just like his father. It is reflected in everything he did and does. After he became the president of the United States, his focus stayed same. Compassionate conservatism is the core of his administration's policy.

There is a difference between a successful person and a great person. You might be a great human being and at the same time successful. But being successful does not make someone a great human being. Respect, trust, and leadership have to be earned. Having all the money in the world, or being best in your field is not enough to make someone as a great person.

What do we have to do as parents to ensure the success of our children, not only in their careers, but also in their lives? We need to help our children to build their character. Teach them to be compassionate. Teach our child to be attentive and empathetic to others. Provide them opportunities to help others in need. One way to do this is by signing them up for a volunteer activity.

I want to introduce *Paradoxical Ten Commandments of Leadership* by Kent M. Keith. (These Commendments were written as part of his book, *The Silent Revolution: Dynamic Leadership in the Student Council*, published in 1968 by Harvard Student Agencies, Cambridge, MS. © Copyright Kent M. Keith 1968, renewed 2001. Used by permission.)

1. People are illogical, unreasonable, and self-centered.
   Love them anyway.
2. If you do good, people will accuse you of
   selfish ulterior motives. Do good, anyway.
3. If you are successful, you will win false friends
   and true enemies. Succeed anyway.
4. The good you do today will be forgotten tomorrow.
   Do good anyway.
5. Honesty and frankness make you vulnerable.
   Be honest and frank anyway.
6. The biggest men and women with the biggest ideas can be shot
   down by the smallest men and women with the smallest minds.
   Think big anyway.

7. People favor underdogs but follow only top dogs. Fight for a few underdogs anyway.
8. What you spend years building may be destroyed overnight. Build anyway.
9. People really need help and may attack you if you do help them. Help people anyway.
10. Give the world the best you have and you'll get kicked in the teeth. Give the world you have anyway.

Always remember your life is more than climbing the ladder to the top. Teach your children to be compassionate. Teach them the value of giving and serving others. It might not promise great wealth or reward, but remember; it will enable them to become a spectacular success in something called life.

11.

Develop Winning Personality Traits through Trials and Difficulties

"There is nothing to fear but fear itself."   *(Franklin D. Roosevelt)*

On May 2nd, 1997, Franklin Roosevelt's Memorial was dedicated in Washington, D.C. Franklin Roosevelt led the World War II victory and saved the nation from the Great Depression. At first, when the Roosevelt Memorial was built, it was to represent not only the president but also the era he represented. It was to celebrate the success of the New Deal program, the end of the Great Depression and the World War II. It portrayed his success as the president of the United States, but fail to depict his personal side, his struggle and triumphant as a fellow human being. The statue of him in his wheel chair was dedicated almost four years later, on January 10, 2001 by then President Clinton.

Roosevelt was born January 30, 1882, at his parent's lavish estate in Springwood, New York. He was the only child born to James Roosevelt and Sara Delano Roosevelt. His mother, who would become a strong influence on the president-to-be throughout his lifetime, supervised his early education until he was fourteen years old. Considering his background, it is amazing how much he did for the common men and women. If he did not have his disability, this might never have happened.

On August 9th, 1921, while sailing near his summer home on Campobello Island, Roosevelt fell into the cool waters. He was diagnosed as polio. He exercised frequently and used swimming a to help regain some movement in his legs. Later, he heard of a retreat in Warm Springs, Georgia, where similar polio patients had found some relief from their ailments. Roosevelt would spend a great amount of time at Warm Springs, relaxing and swimming in the pool of warm mineral water. He devoted not only his time, but also large amounts of his family fortune in an attempt to discover a cure for his disease. He eventually purchased the property and spent so much of his time there; it came to be known as the "little White House." Although his hard work and dedication lifted the nation from poverty and guided it through war, it failed him in his quest to regain the use of his legs. Until the day he died, he was in his wheel chair.

Franklin Roosevelt led a struggle throughout his presidency for assisting "the Forgotten Man." His transformation was only possible because of his disability. As Roosevelt fought against the debilitating disease, he saw first-hand those struggling people who were not able to afford the best doctors and the finest facilities. In response, he funded a polio rehabilitation center in Warm Springs to help those who could not help themselves. This experience continued to influence Roosevelt as he led the country through the crisis of the Great Depression.

At his second inauguration, Roosevelt commented that he saw one third of the nation "ill-housed, ill clad, and ill-nourished." Faced with the daunting task of lifting the country out of a crippling depression, Roosevelt traveled the nation speaking to farmers who had lost all their possessions, meeting with relief organizations overburdened by the demands of those in need and addressing the fears of people struggling to survive. What the American people saw was a man with whom they had little in common, who exhibited sympathy, understanding, and reassurance. It was all made possible because of his disability.

On his statue Eleanor Roosevelt wrote, "His illness made him stronger. He learned to empathize and to be patient." There is a great story about how patient he was. One day, President Roosevelt's second son was walking down the White House hallway and saw that the light in his office was still on. He thought it was odd; after all it was way past midnight. He knocked on the door and walked into find his father still sitting in his office. President Roosevelt's bodyguard fell asleep while waiting for president to finish his work. Roosevelt did not want to wake his bodyguard, so he was patiently waiting for him to wake up and take him up to his bedroom. Of course, that bodyguard got fired the next day, but it shows how patient he was.

Franklin Delano Roosevelt is a hero of the twentieth century. His Memorial in Washington, D.C. is an evidence of it. He is the only president in twentieth century to have his own Memorial. He was patient and learned to appreciate what less fortunate people had to go through everyday. He became "The People's President."

Roosevelt was one of the most successful presidents in American history. As he entered the White House in 1933, he inherited a crippled country. But his New Deal program made those less fortunate able to provide a living for themselves. He founded the United Nations. No one will dispute his success as a president, but his achievement as a human being was greater. He overcame his disability and used it as a tool of empathy. He had to overcome numerous obstacles to become what he was. He suffered from polio that left him in a wheel chair till the day he died. His rehabilitation process was long and painful, but he endured and was able to stand up for his country, even in his wheel chair. He was a fighter. He was a winner. He could have fallen deep into self-pity; instead, he overcame his disability with a challenging spirit. His attitude made a difference, not just in him, but the world around him.

Time magazine selects a "person of the year" at the end of every year. However, to celebrate the turn of the 21st century and look back at how much we have changed, *Time* decide to run a special "the person of the century" issue instead. Many, including then President Bill Clinton expected the former President Roosevelt, who rescued the United States from the Great Depression of the 1930s and who led the World War II to victory, would be selected as the "person of the twentieth century" for sure. There were several reasons that many believed that President Roosevelt would be the one.

First of all, Roosevelt was selected as *Time* Magazine's person of the year in 1922. Because of his great achievements historical society considered him one of the greatest presidents of the United States since Abraham Lincoln. Even though, many thought Roosevelt would win the title, President Clinton and the National Organization on Disability, where I had the privilege to work, put in extra effort to help others, including *Time* magazine to realize the great achievements of the Roosevelt. President Clinton and many influential members of the community wrote letters to the editors of *Time* letting them know how great President Roosevelt was. Every letter written praised President Roosevelt not only as great leader of one country, but also as a great man who worked tirelessly for his beliefs. On top of that, to promote Roosevelt, the National Organization on Disability raised thirty thousand dollars to place an ad in *Time*. The caption read, "Not disability but only ability." Everybody, especially myself, thought Roosevelt would win for sure. If someone asked me to place a bet on it, I wouldn't have hesitated.

Finally, December, 1999 came and *Time* magazine announced "the person of the twentieth century." Roosevelt lost the title to Albert Einstein. I was stunned. According to the news I heard on that evening, *Time* picked Albert Einstein because he paved the way for the modern technological innovations since 1990s, which will continue to affect us in the next centuries. Later I also found out that Thomas Edison won the title of "the nineteenth century person of the century." President Lincoln lost the title to Edison.

What do Albert Einstein and Thomas Edison have in common? To many, it might be an incomprehensible irony, but both of these incredible geniuses had learning disabilities. How can it be? It is easier than you might think. You might not realize it, but you see it everyday. We see great violin players who cannot throw a ball a cross the room. One child may do exceptionally well in English without even trying, but do absolutely horrible in math even though he or she spends all day studying.

Renowned psychologist Joy Paul Guilford divided intelligence into subdimensions. In Guilford's structure of intellect theory (SI), intelligence is viewed as comprised of operations, contents, and products. There are five kinds of operations: cognition, memory, divergent production, convergent production, and evaluation: There are six kinds of products: units, classes, relations, systems, transformations, and implications. There are five kinds of contents: visual, auditory, symbolic, semantic, behavioral. Since each of these dimensions is independent, there are theoretically 150 different components of intelligence. While it is impossible to do exceedingly well in every aspect of intelligence, it is possible we can do exceptionally well in certain aspects. This is how a fool and a genius can co-exist perfectly within a person.

Now, it is given that Einstein and Edison were geniuses and intellectually gifted. But their road to success was not an easy journey.

Albert Einstein was born in a Jewish family who lived in Germany. Around 1886, he began his school career and his violin lessons in Munich. His mother taught him Judaism at home. Two years later he entered the Luitpold Gymnasium. There, problems started. His language development lagged behind compared to his peers. He missed many classes. That was one of the contributing factors of his poor performance in school. His grades were bad. He had problems concentrating on his schoolwork. Soon, he was labeled as a problematic child. In search of a better education, his worried parents moved him to different schools. The entire family had to move to town after town in the search of a better educational environment for young Albert. But, it didn't work. His grades continued to suffer. In 1895, Einstein failed an examination that would have allowed him to study for a diploma as an electrical engineer at the Eidgenoessische Technische Hochschule (ETH) in Zurich. Following the failing of the entrance exam to the ETH, Einstein attended secondary school at Aarau, planning to use this route to enter the ETH. While at Aarau, he wrote an interesting essay about his plans for the future, for which he was only given a little above half marks:

If I were to have the good fortune to pass my examinations, I would go to Zurich. I would stay there for four years in order to study mathematics and physics. I imagine myself becoming a teacher in those branches of the natural sciences, choosing the theoretical part of them. Here are the reasons that lead me to this plan. Above all, it is my disposition for abstract and mathematical thought, and my lack of imagination and practical ability.

Indeed Einstein succeeded with his plan of graduating in 1900 as a teacher of mathematics and physics. One of his friends at ETH was Marcel Grossmann, who was in the same class as Einstein. Einstein tried to obtain a post, writing to Hurwitz who held out some hope of a position but nothing came of it. Three of Einstein's fellow students, including Grossmann, were appointed assistants at ETH in Zurich, but Einstein had not impressed ETH enough.

In 1901, Einstein wrote to universities in the hope of obtaining a job, but without success. Then, Grossmann's father tried to help Einstein to get a job by recommending him to the director of the patent office in Bern. Einstein was appointed as a third-class technical expert. How did the problematic child who failed a college entrance exam, a clerk at the patent office, not only manage to achieve his goal, teaching science, but also become "the person of the twentieth century?" How did he do it? We will get back to it shortly, right after meeting another famous problem child, Thomas Edison.

Thomas Edison was born on February 11, 1847, to middle-class parents in the bustling port of Milan, Ohio, a large wheat-shipping community. In 1854, his family moved to Port Huron, Michigan. Edison's language skills developed slowly. Surprisingly, Edison did not learn to talk until he was almost four years old. Immediately thereafter, he began pleading with everyone he met to explain the workings of just about everything he encountered. If someone said they didn't know, he would look them straight in their eyes, with his deeply set and vibrant blue-green eyes, and ask them "Why?"

When Thomas Edison started school, it could not satisfy his curiosity. At age seven—after spending twelve weeks in a noisy one-room schoolhouse with thirty-eight other students of all ages—Tom's overworked and short-tempered teacher finally lost his patience with the child's relatively self-centered behavior and persistent questioning. Noting that Tom's head was "slightly larger than average," he made no secret of his belief that the hyperactive youngster's brain were "addled" or scrambled.

If modern psychology had existed then, Tom would have probably been deemed a victim of ADS (attention deficit syndrome) and prescribed a hefty dose of the "miracle drug" Ritalin. Instead, when his beloved mother became aware of the situation, she promptly withdrew him from school and began to teach at home. Edison once said, his mom "was the making of me... and was always so true and so sure of me, I felt I had someone to live for... and was someone I must not disappoint

How did Edison do it? He got very little formal education. He once was labeled as "addled." He couldn't even talk until he was four years old. Yet, he invented the light bulb, phonographs, and numerous other inventions. He obtained 1,093 patents, which is still the world's record. What made him such a spectacular success? It is pretty hard, if not impossible, for someone who has doctorate degrees in sciences or technology to have one patent, but here is a person who only had three months of formal education and holds the world record for patents. What was so different for him?

Both Albert Einstein and Thomas Edison had parents who were committed to their children's education. Albert Einstein's parents moved several times to find him a better school. It might seem like a small sacrifice to make for ones child. But every parent knows that it isn't. Moving does not mean just finding a new place to live, which is a big hassle in itself. It also means getting a new job. Everything has to be re-adjusted. Einstein's parents were willing to do anything for their son's education.

Edison also had parents who were devoted to his education. Edison's mother, Nancy Edison, was a descendant of the prominent Elliot family of New England, the devout daughter of a highly respected Presbyterian minister, and an educator in her own right, who commenced teaching her last and favorite son the "Three Rs" and the Bible. Meanwhile, his rather roguish and "worldly" father, Samuel, was more inclined toward having him master the great classics, giving Thomas a ten cent reward for each one he completed.

Of course, having wonderful parents to guide their way was crucial to the success of Einstein and Edison, but it was not the only reason. Their secret to success, the most crucial factor that decided their success was their attitude. Their optimism toward their surroundings and their life was the reason for their success. Both of them saw the world with wonder in their eyes. Einstein's unquenchable curiosity and thirst for knowledge led him to the theory of the relativity. And Thomas Edison's curiosity for life never went away even after he grew up. He wanted to know. He wanted to learn. That was why he could not give up after failing thousands of experiments. He had to go on even after thousands of failures. His famous quote; "1 percent inspiration and 99 percent perspiration" led to more inventions than we can name.

Values such as an optimism, persistence, and perseverance can be learned. Former psychology professor at the University of Chicago, Benjamin Bloom identified three domains (categories) of educational activities. The three domains are cognitive, affective, and psychomotor. The cognitive domain involves knowledge and the development of intellectual skills. This includes recall or recognition of specific facts, procedural patterns, and concepts that serve in the development of intellectual abilities and skills. The psychomotor domain includes physical movement, coordination, and use of the motor-skill areas. Development of these skills requires practice and is measured in terms of speed, precision, distance, procedures, or techniques in executions. The affective domain includes the manner in which we deal with things emotionally, such as feelings, values, appreciation, enthusiasms, motivations, and attitudes. Edison and Einstein were motivated, persistent, enthusiastic, and positive people. They were successful because their abilities in affective domain were high.

We just saw two great persons who succeeded. But, in truth, everyday we see many people with great intellectual abilities are failing miserably. Children with degrees from prestigious colleges do not know what to do after they graduate. Why is that? It's because success is not determined by intellectual ability alone. According to the research conducted by U.S. Department of Education, more than half of the once gifted children now live as underachievers. On the flip side, Professor Joseph F. Ranzulli of the University of Connecticut showed that children with average or higher intellectual abilities can be successful, if they are motivated and focused. In other words, even if your children are not little geniuses in his or her school, he or she can be spectacularly successful, if he or she is focused and willing to work hard for it. In a way, abilities in the affective domain might be more important than the ones in the cognitive domain.

What if Edison had not such persistence? What if he just gave up and accepted the label that his teacher stuck on his forehead? We might still be sitting under oil lamps, or waiting weeks to hear from our relatives who live across the state line. What if Einstein gave up after failing the entrance exam? What if he gave up on physics and settled down as a patent clerk? The world would be a different place. Developing the abilities of the affective domain is vital to success. Then how do we help our children? What do we have to do as parents?

The first step is to teach our children how to concentrate on what they do and how to manage their time. My son Paul worked as an admissions officer at Phillips Exeter for a year before he went off to medical school. Thanks to him, I could gain some insights of applicants of that school and their academic progress afterward. Even though applicants had excellent intellectual abilities, if they did not know how to manage their time, and don't know how to concentrate on what they are doing in that very moment, they failed miserably. Failures generally cause them to retract, and soon they tend to easily give up whatever they were doing.

Knowing how to manage time and the ability to concentrate are "learned behaviors." If you practice them again and again, you can improve those things dramatically. The problem is that you cannot learn them while you are stuck in the classroom all day. At Phillips Academy, students attend classes for thirty weeks. They go to school five days a week. Classes start at eight o'clock in the morning and end at two fifteen. Between two thirty to four o'clock, students are required to participate in after-school activities. It might be sports, volunteer work, newspapers, etc. After-school activities might cause your son or daughter to loose a point or two on a math test, at first. But in the long run, those activities will be beneficial. Finally, students study independently after dinner. Compared to public schools, students spend less time studying. Despite that fact, they firmly hold the reputation as "the best school" in the nation. Of course, they have excellent academic programs, but the reason for their student's success could be found in these after-school activities, too. Students of these schools learned to concentrate on what they are doing. They study hard and play hard. Because they know they have limited time to do everything, they also know that they have to manage their time efficiently. Managing their own schedules not only gives them freedom, but also makes them responsible for their actions. Burdens, such as taking responsibility for their choices, help them to develop their minds.

The second step is to help our children to believe in themselves. We have to help our children to be confident. They have to believe in themselves, believe in what they are doing to be persistent and be successful in their lives. It happened when Paul went to Duke University Hospital to start his residency. He told me, "Without your conviction that I am intellectually gifted, current success would not have been possible. At that time, I didn't believe you, but it has been proven that I was wrong and you were right." What he told me was so touching, I almost cried. I believed in Paul's ability. I always believed he could do it. Despite the fact that I always knew he would be successful, not giving up on him was not easy. Of course, the burden was mostly upon Paul, but seeing Paul's struggle was almost unbearable. Sometimes, I thought that it might be better for Paul to just do whatever he can and just enjoy his life. From time to time, I even thought that putting Paul in the gifted Children's program was my selfish desire. But every time I wanted to give up on Paul, I remembered the stories of Einstein, Edison, Helen Keller, and Miss Sullivan, and especially the stories of Abraham Lincoln and his son. These stories gave me the strength to hold on to our dreams.

Because of his love for learning, Lincoln was also interested in the education of his sons. His devotion to his beloved first son Robert Todd was noteworthy. While Lincoln was still in Springfield, Ill., he sent Robert to England to study. Robert was a bright young man. He got accepted to England's most prestigious preparatory school, Eton School. But, once he got there he could not handle the school. It was not because he did not have the ability to succeed. He was not focused; he did not know how to manage his time effectively. During the three semesters that he spent at Eton School, he failed seventeen subjects. Instead of giving up on him, Lincoln brought Robert back home to Illinois. He made him attend Illinois State University in Springfield, which was a preparatory school with four instructors. Apparently the studies were not difficult. In Robert's own words, "We did just what pleased us, study consuming only a portion of our time." Still he was not motivated. He was not focused. The result was a miserable failure. In 1859, he applied to Harvard, but he failed its entrance examinations. It was apparent his educational abilities were deficient. Again, Lincoln did not give up. He looked for a better school that would develop not only his intellectual abilities but also teach Robert to be persistent and to challenge himself. Lincoln found the perfect school. He sent Robert to Phillips Exeter Academy. Lincoln visited Robert to encourage him. In 1860, Robert was accepted at Harvard and later became a lawyer.

Robert Lincoln had his father, Abraham, and my son Paul had me. Sometimes, children need helping hands to realize their potential. Sometimes, just faintly knowing what they can do it is not enough. To be successful, children have to be persistent. They should keep trying and never give up. To be persistent, children have to believe in themselves. But one more thing we have to keep in mind. In order to help them to believe in themselves, we have to believe in them first.

The third step is to help children find their goals in life. Without goals, there is no reason for them trying harder and being persistent. Winston Churchill was a man who never gave up on himself. He overcame many obstacles throughout his life. The twentieth century produced six politicians who will be remembered by the coming generations: Lenin, Stalin, Hitler, Mao Zedong, Franklin Roosevelt, and Winston Churchill. The first four were totalitarians, Roosevelt and Churchill differed from them because they believed in democracy. And Churchill differed from Roosevelt—while both were war leaders, Churchill was uniquely stirred by the challenge of war and found his fulfillment in leading the democracies to victory.

After the war, Churchill wrote a book *History of the Second World War*, and won the Nobel Prize for literature. As a great leader, a successful politician, and a award-winning writer, it was expected that when he gave a speech it would be a long and elaborate oratory. But, on October 29, 1941, when he visited Harrow School to hear the traditional songs he used to sing there as a youth, and to speak to the students, there, instead of a long-winded speech, he got up and gave a one-sentence speech that later became one of his most-quoted speeches of all times. He walked up to the podium and said, "Never, ever, ever, ever, ever give up." That was it. Maybe all he had to say about his success was just that: Never give up on anything.

Winston Churchill was a great leader. He was a great writer. But he wasn't a great success at the beginning. What made him such a successful person? What was his secret? After all, *Time* magazine does not name anybody from down the block as the person of the half-century.

Winston Churchill was born in November 30, 1874, to Lord Randolph Churchill, a conservative politician and Jennie Jerome, the daughter of a New York businessman. Churchill stuttered and spoke with a lisp. Because of his stuttering, he was considered to have a learning disability, just like our fellow winners of the "person of the century" title, Einstein and Edison. He also was a terrible student. In his early years as a student, he got straight F's. As a young man of undistinguished academic accomplishment—he was admitted to Sandhurst after failing twice—he finally managed to enter the army as a cavalry officer. His father despised him because of his constant failures. He once wrote to Winston's grandmother, the dowager

Duchess of Marlborough, that the boy lacked cleverness, knowledge, and any capacity for settled work. He has a great talent for show-off, exaggeration, and make believe. How did he become a great leader and win the Nobel Prize?

Looking back, his life was full of accomplishments. But when you look into his life for more than five minuets, you can quickly notice what he had to do to overcome his numerous obstacles. It was his persistence, his positive outlook on his life, and support from his wife. He summarized his life-long pursuit of success in one sentence. His secret to success was persistence. In order to say, "never give up," can you imagine how many failures that he had to endure?

Of course, he had to deal with many personal problems such as his father's disapproval and his stuttering. But his career path also was paved with many failures. Churchill entered Parliament in 1901 at age twenty-six. In 1904, he left the Conservative Party to join the Liberals, in part out of calculation: the Liberals were the coming party, and in its ranks he soon achieved high office. He became home secretary in 1910 and first lord of the admiralty in 1911. Thus it was as political head of the Royal Navy at the outbreak of the First World War in 1914 that he stepped onto the world stage.

As a passionate believer in the navy's historic strategic role, he immediately committed the Royal Naval Division to an intervention in the Flanders campaign in 1914. Frustrated by the stalemate in Belgium and France that followed, he initiated the allies' only major effort to outflank the Germans on the Western front by sending the navy, and later a large force of the army, to the Mediterranean. At Gallipoli in 1915, this Anglo-French force struggled to break the defenses that blocked access to the Black Sea. It was a heroic failure that forced Churchill's resignation and led to his political eclipse.

In 1924, he rejoined the Conservatives. The Conservative prime minister appointed Churchill as the Chancellor of the Exchequer, but when he returned the country to the gold standard, it proved financially disastrous, and he further weakened his political position by opposing measures to grant India limited self-government. He resigned office in 1931 and entered what appeared to be a terminal political decline. But he faced the biggest challenge during the World War II. During 1935, he not only warned the House of Commons about the importance of self-preservation, but also the preservation of free governments against the ever advancing sources of authority and despotism. His anti-

Bolshevik policies had failed. By espousing anti-Nazi policies in his wilderness years between 1933 and 1939, he ensured that the moment of final confrontation between Britain and Hitler in 1940. He stood out as the one man in whom the nation could place its trust.

Following the total defeat of France, Britain truly, in his words, "stood alone." Britain had no substantial allies and, for much of 1940, lay under the threat of German invasion and under constant German air attacks. He nevertheless refused Hitler's offers of peace. He organized a successful air defense that led to victory in the Battle of Britain. And he, meanwhile, sent most of what remained of the British army, after its escape from the humiliation of Dunkirk, to the Middle East to oppose Hitler's Italian ally, Mussolini.

From the outset of his premiership, Churchill, half American by birth, had rested his hope of ultimate victory in U.S. intervention. He had established a personal relationship with President Roosevelt with whom he hoped a war-winning alliance. Roosevelt's reluctance to commit the U.S. beyond an association short of war did not dent his optimism. He always hoped events would work his way. The decision by Japan, Hitler's ally, to attack the American Pacific fleet at Pearl Harbor on Dec. 7, 1941, justified his hopes. That evening he confided to himself, "So we had won after all."

His name had been made, and he stood unchallengeable, as the greatest of all Britain's war leaders. It was not only his own country that owed him a debt, so too did the world of free men and women to whom he had made a constant and inclusive appeal in his magnificent speeches, "never, ever, ever give up."

Churchill once said that the wisest decision he ever made was to marry his wife Clementine. She believed in him and gave him strength when he wanted to give up. In one of his letters to his wife, he wrote: "Time passes swiftly, amid the storms and stresses of so many events when he is with his wife." He made it clear that support from his wife Clementine was vital to his success.

Extraordinary people are not born, they are made. First with proper goals and visions for one self, then followed with persistent effort. And remember, like Oprah Winfrey once said, "Nobody makes it alone." Everybody needs someone to guide him or her through the tough times. Be your children's guide and strength. Teach them to be persistent. And don't forget the words of one ordinary person who became an extraordinary success, "never, ever ever give up."

12.

Surround Yourself With People Who Have the Same Goals and Values

Power does not come from a position, but it comes from what you believe in.   *(George W. Bush)*

Everyday, when we turn on the news, when we open the newspapers, and when we open the magazines, we hear the term "globalization." Thanks to great technological innovations, we can now talk and see a person in the middle of jungle, if we really want to. We can buy and sell stocks of companies in Japan. Countries in Europe now use the Euro.

Students can learn about other cultures without ever leaving their classrooms. Everything is international. Everything is global. The world is getting smaller every minute. Boarders are disappearing in front of our very eyes. Boarders, which once stood firmly in businesses and cultures are now becoming political terms that exist in books only. And, we are standing in the midst of a fast-changing world. So, a question is who can rise up to face the new-found challenges of globalization and become a true leader?

Some say that Americans are self-centered and arrogant, but it is not really wrong to say, "Globalization means Americanization." It is not intended to be an ethnocentric statement. It simply means that the influences of United States on the world economy and cultures are greater than other countries around the world. Who, then, moves America? America is referred to as a great melting pot. The cultural and racial diversity is one of the unique gifts that contribute so much to our success. While it is impossible to decide which group of people contributed most, one group surely stands out.

There are six million Jewish Americans in the United States. While they make up only 3 percent of the population, according to *Jewish-American Today* by Charles E. Silberman, fifteen out of twenty-one so-called elites of our society are Jewish Americans. The leader of financial world, Alan Greenspan, is a Jew. Their leadership does not stop there. There are several outstanding Jewish American politicians in many government positions: to name a few; former secretary of treasury, Robert Rubin; former secretary of state, Madeline Albright; former secretary of defense, William Cohen. This notable phenomenon fascinates not only the public, but also many in the fields of education and psychology. One of them is Arthur Jensen from Stanford University. He conducted and compared the results of intelligence test between many racial and social groups. From his research, he found that the intellectual abilities of Jewish Americans are not greater than any other ethnic group in America. Then, what makes such difference? The answer can be found in their early education.

The role of mothers in the Jewish family is well known. They play pivotal roles in the future success of their children. Up until their kids reach age thirteen, Jewish mothers instill in their children traditional values. They not only teach them to work hard, but they also teach them to be persistent and learn from their mistakes and failures. They not only teach them the values of their old world, but they also teach them the values of their present world. Many educators and psychologists found the reason for much of the success of Jews around the world stems from their early education. Unlike other ethnic groups, they were able to preserve their own traditional values while adapting the values of the new world. Because their firm grip on their value system, they were able to become new leaders of the world.

Then, what kinds of values must be instilled in our children? When should we begin? It is always best to start value education early in the lives of children. It is more effective, and it will probably last a lifetime. One question remains; because values are subjective matters, we really cannot say which values are better than others. If one tries, value can be placed in different categories. Even though, it is possible to put one value under the heading of one category, the distinction is not really clear. One particular value can be placed in more than one category. One value can conflict with other values. It would be wonderful if values were clear-cut and we could decide which value is the ultimate value, but in reality it is impossible.

So, what are the values? First, there are "universal" values. "Universal" values include freedom, liberty, life, autonomy, etc. These values are considered important regardless of our races, ages, religions, and nationalities. Second, there are "particular" values. These values are related to specific cultures. Respecting your elders can be a simple illustration. Asian countries have a different sense of respect toward elders. They respect their elders not because they have to, but because they have the wisdom that comes with life-long experiences. While, in the Western world, elders are valued as obsolete who are no longer productive members of society, in Asia they are respected as essential members of society, as teachers who can teach their next generation, as experts who have wisdom and expertise of life, which only comes with age. Third, there are also "terminal" and "instrumental" values. Terminal values include honesty, equality, and peace, which we want to achieve and preserve. Instrumental values include honesty, and forgiveness. It is important to have the right instrumental values, but the instrumental values are only mere tools to the reach the end of terminal values.

Americans value self-respect, equality, peace, happiness, safety, and fame as terminal values. And Americans value honesty and compassion, responsibility, forgiveness, and obedience as instrumental values. The founding fathers of the United States came to this new land in search of religious freedom, therefore, most traditional American values stem from the Bible. Some of these values are reflected in the policies of the Bush administration. These policies and values include freedom, dignity, equality, compassion, and inclusion. These ideas originated from the biblical concept that we are created equal in God's image and the story of Good Samaritan from the Bible.

Some values, such as money and religion, can be instrumental values for some, but at the same time they can be terminal values for others. Values conflict with each other. No one has complete freedom to do whatever they desire to do. Sometimes, ones freedom has to be limited to some degree to ensure the safety of others. It might seem confusing, but one thing still remains; as parents, we should instill proper values in our children.

This seemingly difficult task is actually quiet simple. First and most important, parents must be proper role models. Children are white linen that absorbs every color in their surroundings. Being a good example is better than nonstop nagging. If you want your children to grow up to be honest men and women, you have to be honest first. If you want to teach children to respect themselves, you have to respect yourself and others around you.

Second, we have to read to them books with great values. While it is critical to start planting values in our children, it is hard for them to actually grasp the concept of each value or have meaningful discussions about them. The most effective way to show children the importance of values would be reading them stories. It might be a bedtime story or story from the Bible. You can read them the story of the tortoise and the hare to teach them about the importance of persistence. You can read them the story of the Good Samaritan to teach them about compassion.

Value education is most effective if you start early in a child's life, but it does not mean there is no hope if we start to educate them about it when they are older. Also, education about values should not stop when children reach a certain age; it should be reinforced and reminded continuously throughout their lives. Once children reach young adulthood, the education styles should be changed along with them. Now, children can somewhat understand the concept of each value. They can have a fairly good discussion. Also, they can find role models by themselves. One of the best ways for them to do so is through books.

No one on earth can experience everything. But we can experience so many different aspects of our lives through books. There are heroes and villains. There are not only fights between good and evil but also inner conflicts of values. Through books, children can experience almost anything. The University of Chicago is one of great institutions that succeeded in teaching value education to young adults.

The University of Chicago is referred to as the "Land of Nobel Prizes." In its relative short history, its academic success is remarkable. When the University of Chicago opened its door on 1890, it has to face many challenges. Its location was not so great. Most of the best students around the country attended Ivy League schools. Until 1929, the University of Chicago was just a school in Chicago. But everything changed once Robert Hutchinson became the president of the university. He accomplished many great things for school, but what transformed the University of Chicago from a second-tiered school to the land of the Nobel Prize was his "Great Books Project." The Great Books Project, which requires every student at the University of Chicago to read at least one hundred great books in order to graduate, was great success. It was his belief that, through books, young adults can discover not only whole new worlds of possibilities, but also values that will affect them for the rest of their lives. His effort did not just stop there. He even demolished the gym to build a library. Almost eighty years later, more than seventy university professors who graduated from the University of Chicago received Nobel Prizes, and the university has world-renowned academic programs that compete with Ivy League schools.

For every parent, the values that we chose for our children and for ourselves can be different, but we have to remember that the values we choose will follow our children for the rest of their lives. As parents, we also have to recognize that values sometimes conflict. We have to teach our children not only to have proper values, but also to show them how to deal with the inner conflicts they will face everyday due to those values.

Having proper values is the first step to success, but it is not the end. Even if you are truly gifted and have values that can hold you tight in stormy days, if nobody knows about them, they are useless. Everybody needs somebody that will help him or her along the way. Knowing the right people at the right time is an essential ingredient to success.

One of my nieces told me that the first thing she learned in business school was the importance of networking. She said from the first day until the day she graduated from college, the term "networking" was instilled in every student in school. Also, business students are encouraged to join clubs and various activities and to become leaders in those organizations. One might say, "Of course! If you want to be in business, you have to build networks that work for you." But, the truth of the matter is that to be successful in any field, you need to have "networks." It is not only for people in business, but also true for everybody; dentists have the ADA (American Dental Association); and doctors have the AMA (American Medical Association). Doctors, dentists, and many other professionals are encouraged to join professional organizations and are told to "network" in the first day of their school. For me, networking conveys more than meeting colleagues, making friends, or joining the professional organizations. Networking is a channel and a tool that communicates our values and beliefs to others.

Whether we like it or not, human beings are social animals. From the moment we are born, we are somebody's son or daughter. We are somebody's grandchild. We are the annoying brother or sister of someone. The moment we take our first breath, we become a part of a family and a society.

In 1999, on Thanksgiving Day, a little boy from Cuba stunned the American public. The fate of Elian Gonzalez, a six-year-old boy, became a worldwide controversy after being rescued by a fisherman off the coast of Florida. He was one of three survivors on a boat fleeing Cuba. The boat capsized, and his mother, stepfather, and eight others died. Elian's relatives in the U.S and anti-Castro Cuban Americans wanted him to stay in America, claiming his life would be better than in communist Cuba. They also wanted to honor his mother's dying wish. But his father, a hotel worker in Cuba, demanded the boy's return, and Fidel Castro's government joined the custody battle, calling on thousands of demonstrators throughout the island nation to march on the father's behalf. Days later, the U.S. Immigration and Naturalization Service said that the father should have custody of the boy.

Like Elian, we are pretty much stuck with our families and societies. It would be wonderful if we could interview our parents before we were born, but we don't have that choice. Even though we cannot decide where we want to belong at first, we still don't know what Elian really wanted for himself, as we get older, we gain more control over our destiny. And eventually, we can decide where to join in or not to join.

Because we are social beings and we have wants and needs to belong, we look for friends and companionship. There are two different kinds of friends. It is not boyfriends and girlfriends. It is not good friends and bad friends. It depends on how you meet each other and the purpose of your friends you can divide friends into two different groups. The first group of friends is "coincidental friends." You meet these friends by luck and coincidence. You do not plan to meet these friends. These are friends from school, friends from your old neighborhood. These are the buddies that you sit next to on the school bus. These are the friends who made silly faces with in your youth. The other group of friends is "intentional friends." You meet these friends when you join certain kinds of activities or clubs. These friends share similar goals and values. These are the friends that you meet in the book clubs or local YMCAs while volunteering. These are the friends that you sought out. A long time ago, there were only coincidental friends—where you were born, your family members, and the school you attended. But as world gets smaller everyday, things that once mattered are losing their values. Instead of coincidental friends, the necessities of intentional friends are increasing. It does not mean one particular group of friends is better than the others. It means, to be successful in whatever we, we have to recognize the ever-increasing importance of meeting new people.

But how do you find those great people who share your dreams of goals and values? What do you have to do? First, have a clear goal and intact value system. You have to know what you value most. You have to know what your goals are. If you do not have your own value system, you won't be able to become a leader in any organization. If you do not have your own values to share with others, you are nothing but a mindless drone, riding in the bandwagon. This is why I explained the importance of value education in the begging of the chapter. Once you know what your values and goals are, it is easy to find an organization to join. The organization will become a medium to convey your values and beliefs. And soon, the network that everybody sought after and the prize will emerge without a problem.

I was born in a small country town outside Seoul, Korea. Nothing ever happened there. No rich and famous people ever lived there. I don't think anybody knew ever the phrase "climbing the social latter." I graduated from a school for the blind. Our alumni never had any power over anything. The world was different then. Person with disabilities could not even take the entrance exam to colleges. Disabled people were not allowed to study abroad. The so-called elites, students from the most prestigious universities, were not that different from others regarding the welfare issues of disabled. Christians were not that different from non-Christians.

After studying a year in Yonsei University, one of the oldest schools in Korea, with a full scholarship, I decided to join the school activities to build my character. At that time, I wanted to build my leadership skills. My values were totally focused on self-respect and leadership. I looked into several student organizations that could help me to do what I needed to do. It took me a while to decide where I wanted to join, but I managed to narrow it down to three. One of student organization was Heungsadan, which was one of the oldest student organizations in Korea. Heungsadan's commitment to raising future leaders of Korea is still well known. Another was Noguhoi, which was an intercollegiate organization of students in education major. They were from four different universities in Korea. And lastly, I wanted to join the Students of Christian Association (SCA) that is still an active Christian student organization in Korea. I was eager. I could not wait to join one of those clubs. I wanted to become a leader.

But, none of these clubs accepted me. When I was rejected by SCA, which was the last hope, I decided to start my own student organization with three of my closest friends. They shared my values and dreams. Yes, at first they were my coincidental friends. They were friends who sat next to me in the classroom. They were friends that bumped into me on my way to class. Once, my coincidental friends are now transformed into intentional friends through our little project. We named our organization, "Yonsei Jayoo Kyoyanghoi," and we had our first meeting at my house. Our purpose was to develop leadership skills by reading and discussing classic books. Sometimes, our discussion lasted all night. Through discussions we learned not only about the books, but also learned about each other. When I went back to Korea last August to receive my honorary doctorate in literature, I was thrilled to hear that our club still exists and is flourishing with many great students. Of course, I was glad to hear such great news, but still what I cherish most is the friendships that I shared with my friends in that dark and small room. Because I had such friends who shared my values and goals, I could be where I am right now.

Nothing stays the same. That includes values, too. Values are not stationary. They change as one change over the time. It is impossible to tell whether one changes first then their values change, or one changes because their values are changed. I was not an exception. Since my college years, much has changed. I left my country and moved to America. I met new friends. I learned new things. Those values that my mother instilled in me when I was a young child still remained within me. But what I valued most has been shifted.

When I first came to the United States, I did not have the luxury to help others. It does not mean I forgot about others around me all together. It simply means that I was trying my best to get my degree as soon as possible. I was a new graduate who was struggling to find a job to support my family.

The year 1982 was the beginning of the "OK" period in our marriage, in which we promised God that we would give back and glorify his name through our life together. The first action that I took was to write a book. I wanted to tell my story. I wanted to show the world what God had done for me. I could not have done this much unless God was on my side. But, it was not good enough. I wanted to give back what I have received. What I value most has been changed. I wanted to serve others.

I thought long and hard, and decided to join the Rotary Club. It is a world-renowned service organization. One interesting fact about the Rotary Club is that you have to be invited to join the club. Not every Joe down the street is allowed to join. Even if you got an invitation, it does not guarantee your acceptance. The Rotary Club has a rule. It is placed to ensure the diversity among professionals. For each chapter, every member has to be of a different profession. For example, there can be only one doctor, one dentist, one teacher, one fire fighter, etc. Even if you have an invitation, if the club already has a psychologist and you are a psychologist, you cannot join. Luckily there were no educators on board at the Munster, Indiana, chapter of the Rotary Club. I managed to get an invitation from Williams T. Powell who helped me to get a scholarship from Rotary International many years ago. I told him that I am indebted to the Rotary Club for my success. I told him that I would be a great example for scholarship programs of the Rotary International. I told him that I wanted to serve others through Rotary International.

Once I joined and committed myself to its cause, everything fell into place. I met countless friends who not only helped me but also to taught me so many things. Just seeking an organization and joining it does not equal success. The key is the commitment. You have to commit yourself and do your best to communicate your values and goals. Intentional friends, and great organizations such as Rotary Club, are tools that help you to better yourself. It is not an end in itself. I totally committed myself to its cause.

Because of the Rotary Club, the English version of my book could reach countless Christians all over the nation. Thanks to the Rotary Club, I could meet such great friends like Robert Shuler, Norman Vincent Peale, and Frank Devlin. Because of my background, I only have a handful of coincidental friends. But, former attorney general Thornburgh once said, "Dr. Kang is the most well connected person I ever met." How is that possible? It is because I managed to effectively communicate my values and goals through the Rotary Club. Educator and philosopher John Dewy once said that the relationship between individuals could exist only when there is mutual interest.

Let's meet Frank Devlin, one of my intentional friends. Frank is an international businessman who was born in Mexico. And I am a blind educator who was born in Korea. We have different nationalities. We speak different languages. We have different cultural backgrounds. In a glance, it looks like we have nothing in common, and there is only a remote possibility of us becoming friends on our own. But, we had and still have one thing in common. We both were willing to serve others. We wanted to help others who were less fortunate than us. I met him through Rotary International. He was the person who greeted me with open arms at the Rotary International Convention in 1999 where I had a privilege to give a speech. Our next meeting was at the trustees meeting of the Goodwill Industries.

Between 2000 and 2001, Frank Devlin was elected as the president of the Rotary Club. The president of the Rotary Club has some control over the businesses that the Rotary Club would like to focus on. During his presidency, he led the Rotary Club to focus on rehabilitation of five hundred thousand disabled people around the world. The president's plan was not just focusing on physical rehabilitations. He tried to reintroduce disabled people around the world back into the society as productive members. He wanted to train, educate, and help them to locate jobs. With Goodwill Industries on his side, his project became a great success. Ordinary people do extraordinary works. These ordinary people make history. But no one can do everything by himself or herself. Frank Devlin couldn't have done by himself. And the only reason that I could have taken a part in such extraordinary project was because I shared the vision with Frank.

The word "connections" sometimes has negative connotations. That could be the reason why the term "networking" is more popular these days. Having a connection is not something out of movie. It is not something that TV network executives concocted to make life harder for less-connected people. Making intentional friends does not mean to use your friends for success. It means trying to make friends who share your visions and goals.

Maybe an analogy of streams and rivers might help. Each individual is like a stream that trickles down the rock. While a stream is essential and has its own values to surrounding, it is weak. It is vulnerable to many. It has little power to change its surrounding. But, what happens when these little streams meet other little streams down the mountain? Yes, it becomes a great river. Meeting friends who share the same values and goals is like that. With them on your side, you can do more than you can ever imagine. The values that you communicated with and through them get amplified, and at the end, change the world.

Do you want to raise your children to be successful leaders in this fast-paced new world? Then first, help them to develop their abilities. Spend time with them and found out what their interests, what they are good at. Help them to develop their interests. Second, instill good values. It will not only become an anchor in the midst of ups and downs of their lives, but it will also decide in parts what kinds of people they will become later in their lives. Always, be a proper role model for your child. If you want to see them growing up to be honorable men and women, you have to act like honorable men and women first. Read great books to them. Help them experience as many things as possible through great books. And third, help them to realize the value of intentional friends. Encourage your children to join organizations that share their values and goals. And always remind your children, joining is not the end. Help them become leaders of organization, they have to make a commitment and do their best to communicate their values and goals through the organization.

13.

Love Yourself As You Are: Build Your Identity as a Global Citizen

People become really quite remarkable when they start thinking that they can do things. When they believe in themselves they have the first secret of successes.   *(Norman Vincent Peale)*

On October 4, 1957, the former Soviet Union launched the first satellite, Sputnik I. The world was stunned. The presence of an object orbiting above the United States and Western Europe generated intense anxiety within the defense community and underscored the importance of science and engineering in the further development of technology. The prospect of the Soviet Union developing a long-range missile was frightening. People began to panic. It was just a matter of time. Everybody felt like they were sitting ducks, waiting for the Soviet Union to make the first move. Nobody felt safe. The Russians could bomb anywhere, at any moment. People could not trust their own defense systems. How could they? The Russians can use their satellite to get highly qualified military information, if they want to. The mere possibility and fragments of human imagination lead the nation into panic-stricken chaos. President Eisenhower had to do something. He declared a state of emergency and devised the plans to catch up with the technologies of the Soviet Union.

Meanwhile, then vice president Richard Nixon and Senator John Kennedy were busy with their presidential campaign. On January 20, 1961, John F. Kennedy became the youngest president ever to be elected in United States history. Among the many issues that he had to tackle was a panic-stricken nation lagging behind in technology. How he dealt with these two issues could either make his presidency or break it. When President Kennedy took his office, he addressed the problems the nation was facing in his, now famous inauguration speech:

"My fellow Americans; ask not what your country can do for you, ask what can you do for your country. My fellow citizens of the world: ask not what America will do for you, but what together we can do for the freedom of the man."

Two months later, in the effort to make the world a better place, Kennedy established the Peace Corp, which is still active.

John F. Kennedy was assassinated in November 1963 in Dallas, Texas. He only served two and half years as the president. Even though he did not have enough time to make his legacy as the president, forty years later, he is still considered as one of the best presidents in United States history. Why? Some say that it is because of his speech, which is still etched in the hearts of every American. It is somewhat convincing reason for his popularity, but it has to be more than a single speech. The reason why he is still thought of as one of the greatest Americans in history is not just the speech he delivered alone. It is rather a vision that he presented to America through his powerful words. Before, America was used to its peaceful prosperity. Young people's lives were lax and many lived on aimlessly without a purpose.

But John F. Kennedy changed it all. He instilled such a vision in everybody. For the first time in a long time, countless youth in America found for themselves a purpose in their lives and learned to serve others. For the first time in a long time, Americans put their country and the world first. America woke up from its deep sleep and realized that they could do more and be more. Because of him,

America realized its full potential and started its race toward a better future.

Kennedy was able to ease the fear-stricken Americans into comfort through his unique leadership. At that time, the United State was falling behind in science and technology. While the Soviet Union had a head start on race to the space, the United States was having a massive anxiety attack. What Kennedy did was amazing. Instead of focusing on the race against the Soviet Union, he turned and gave a vision for the future to every American. In other words, he made Americans see that we needed to improve our technology, not to spite the Soviet Union, but to make our country a better place to live, for us and for our future generations.

President Kennedy presented his long-term plans to improve the space program of the United States with firm conviction. He promised, "In ten years, men will walk on the moon." At that time, the United States did not have the technology, nor the budget for his plan. But even after President Kennedy's assassination, his vision lived on. In 1969, two years earlier than his promised date, Neal Armstrong put an American flag on the moon.

14.

Build Self-esteem and Confidence

Through his inauguration speech, President Kennedy changed America. From the educational point of view, he did amazing things for not only for the country as a whole, but also for the youth in general. Kennedy made our younger generation look at themselves. He put pride in them. He made them realize their potential and endless possibilities. He gave them a vision, a goal in their lives. He gave them back the self-respect and self-esteem that are undoubtedly the most crucial factor in human development. According to educational experts, self-image influences success. In other words, how you view yourself affects how you develop your potential. Everybody has immeasurable potential. What you do with it and how do you develop it?

More than once in our lives, we asked ourselves, "Who am I?" "Where am I from? And where am I going?" You don't have to be a philosopher to ponder upon this one simple, yet the most complex question in the history of humanity. Every teenager wonders about it. Every philosopher has searched for it. Some might find their answers in religion. Some will find it in the great books. Some will find it within themselves.

One-third of those who are searching for the ultimate answer for the soul searching questions will confidently say, "I am created in the image of God. That is who I am. God put me on this earth to do God's work. God has a plan for me." There are six billion people on earth, and two billion of them are Christians. You can tell the above figure is pretty accurate.

It is a well-known fact that a person's way of thinking affects his or her self-confidence and self-esteem. William Bennett, the secretary of Education in the Reagan administration, initiated a research project to find the way to boost self-esteem and self-confidence in youth. The findings were what we had known all along. Youth who relate themselves to God had the highest self-esteem and confidence, and achieved higher successes in general.

In other words, the children who were able to relate to God felt they were special indeed. And they also come to believe that they have great potential. On the top of that, children with faith know and believe that it is not mere chance or accident they are here. A sense of purpose is rooted deep down inside of them. They feel the duty and responsibility to do their best early on. In their mind, God did not put them on earth to see life passing by. They are here because God has special plan for each one of them. The right mixture of great self-image, self-respect, and self-esteem, which comes from the sense of privilege and purpose, ensures their success in many aspects of their lives.

When I was a young boy, I lived in the countryside near Seoul. I never liked school. I loved to run around the fields with my friends. And I was way too busy to find out various ways to catch frogs. I was always late for dinner. I never had enough times for homework, but somehow I always managed to find a time for the great game of soccer. Every single day, my mother had to look for me to feed dinner and making me do homework. I think I can still vividly hear her voice:

"Young Woo! Dinner!"

"Nagging" has been an important tool for all parents. My mom wasn't an exception. Whenever I came home from running around with my friends, all muddy and dirty, she started her usual daily lesson. The lesson did not stop until I actually sat down in front of the desk and opened my books. Now, I am too old to remember her repertoire word by word, but she used to say "Study. When are you going to do your homework? I don't want you to become a farmer and stuck here for the rest of your life. It's for your own good. Why can't you study harder?" Sometimes, I wonder why my mom couldn't help me build self-esteem within me, instead of nagging me all the time. I know that it is useless to think about it at this juncture. As an educator, I just wonder. What if she helped me find a better self-image? Would I be different?

According to Jean Piaget, a Swedish child psychologist, there are four primary cognitive development stages: (1) sensory motor, (2) pre-operations, (3) concrete operations, and (4) formal operations. In the sensory motor stage (birth to two years old), the cognitive structure takes the form of motor actions. In the pre-operation period (three to seven years old), the cognitive structure is intuitive. In the concrete operational stage (eight to eleven years old), the cognitive structure is logical, but depends upon concrete referents. In the final stage of formal operations (twelve to fifteen years old), thinking involves abstractions. Every age group processes information differently. It is up to the parents to find the age-appropriate method to their children.

I had a hard time with my two sons. I thought it would be easier for me since this is what I do for a living, but finding specific examples to which they could relate was not an easy task. How can you explain the concept of "potential" to a child who does not even know how to spell the word? How can you explain the concept of doing the best to a child whose biggest challenge is to tie his or her own shoelaces?

I found my answer at the library. One day, all four of us, my wife, Paul, Chris, and I went to a library. We walked through the children's section and picked out some bedtime stories for that week. On the way to the circulation desk, we passed the reference section and decided to look up some famous people who share the same birthdays with us. Paul's birthday is the same day with Shakespeare. Chris' birthday is the same day with Queen Elizabeth II. My wife's birthday is the same day with John F. Kennedy. And I share my birthday with Martin Luther King Jr.

Right after our research, I told my two sons that they could become great people just like Shakespeare and Queen Elizabeth II when they grow up. I did not realized what I had done right away, but soon I could tell I did something great. I could hear my sons' voices rising with excitement. For the next few days, they were busy bragging to their friends about their new findings. They were so proud that they have something in common with such a great people.

There are many heroes and countless great people throughout history. Each one of them has a birthday, just as the rest of us. So, it would not be hard to find someone who was born on your child's birthday. Give them someone with whom they can identify and admire. It will help them to realize their limitless potential.

Several days later, Paul walked up to me with a huge grin on his face. I did not know what he was up to, but I could tell he was excited, and he wanted to tell me something important. I could tell he was going to burst if I just let him stand there a little bit longer. Soon he cracked and shouted out, "Did you know in the year 2000, my birthday is on Easter Sunday? I am sure something great will happen on that day." I guess he found another great person with whom to identify. Fifteen years later, on the Easter Sunday of 2000, we celebrated Paul's graduation from medical school. Something great indeed happened for him; he made his dream come true. He became a doctor that day.

Paul's problem was not his ability, but his self-esteem and confidence. Once Paul started to regain his confidence, he started to believe in himself. He finally began to understand how special he is. Another great change was that Paul began to take initiatives. One day, after school, Paul came up to me and said, "Dad! Would you coach my team?

I thought he was joking. How can I possibly coach baseball or basketball? I told him that I don't think I can coach his team. But Paul insisted, "Dad, I really think you can."

I asked him, "How?"

I could not see him smiling, but I could tell it from his voice. He had a mischievous grin on his face.

"Because." Paul paused for second and said, "It's an academic team. That's why."

Sometimes I felt sorry for my kids. I was not able to play catch with them or coach their little leagues. But Paul gave me a chance to do something about it. I felt so proud and grateful. I became a coach. Who would have known? The academic team that Paul was so excited about was the "Future Problem Solving Program" (FPSP). Originally, E. Paul Torrance developed a program, *The Torrance Test of Creativity Thinking*, to help inner-city kids in Atlanta. FPSP was intended to stimulate critical and creative-thinking skills, and encourage students to develop a vision for their future. Because of its success, FPSP soon became a nationwide competition.

Paul Torrance divided creative ability into four different areas: fluency, flexibility, originality, and elaboration. Each area is subdivided into a verbal and figure section. Together there are eight areas of creative abilities. If one has many ideas, it means he or she has a high fluency. If one can categorize ideas according to the similarities or differences with ease, he or she has high flexibility. If one has unique ideas, he or she has high on originality. Last but not least, elaboration defines the ability, how one develops ideas in detail. The Future Problem Solving Program helps children to develop all four aspects of creativity through realistic problems that children face everyday.

When Paul asked me to coach his team, I jumped at the chance. I already knew and was familiar with FPSP, and its effectiveness, as an educator. But mostly, I did it because I thought it would be a great opportunity to boost Paul's self-confidence. Paul's team won the first place in math in the regional and placed second in the state championship.

It changed Paul's perspective on life and himself. My wife and I told him about it thousand times that he is an intelligent and talented person. We told him that we believed in him. But sometimes hearing is just not enough. In order for him to believe in himself and to be confident, he had to overcome challenges of his own. FPSP was his chance to shine. He finally learned to trust his ability and be confident.

My wife and I wanted our two sons to know that they are Korean Americans and citizens of the world, but more important we wanted them to know that they are precious human beings who were created in the image of God. We wanted them to know that they have limitless possibilities. Helping Paul to find his identity was one of our greatest things we ever did as parents.

Don't nag your children to do their homework. Don't yell at them to study harder. Poor grades and loosing interest in studies could be just symptoms of other problems. Look at them carefully; they might need someone to help them to find themselves. I don't know where

Paul would be if I had gone on doing what I did when he was in third grade. But I am sure he wouldn't be where he is right now.

Remember that "pride" and "arrogance" are different words. Boosting children's self-esteem is not the same as telling them what they want to hear. Remember, confidence and self-respect can be achieved through compassion and understanding others.